KAISER colour

cats & dogs

COLOURING BOOK

40 cat and dog designs

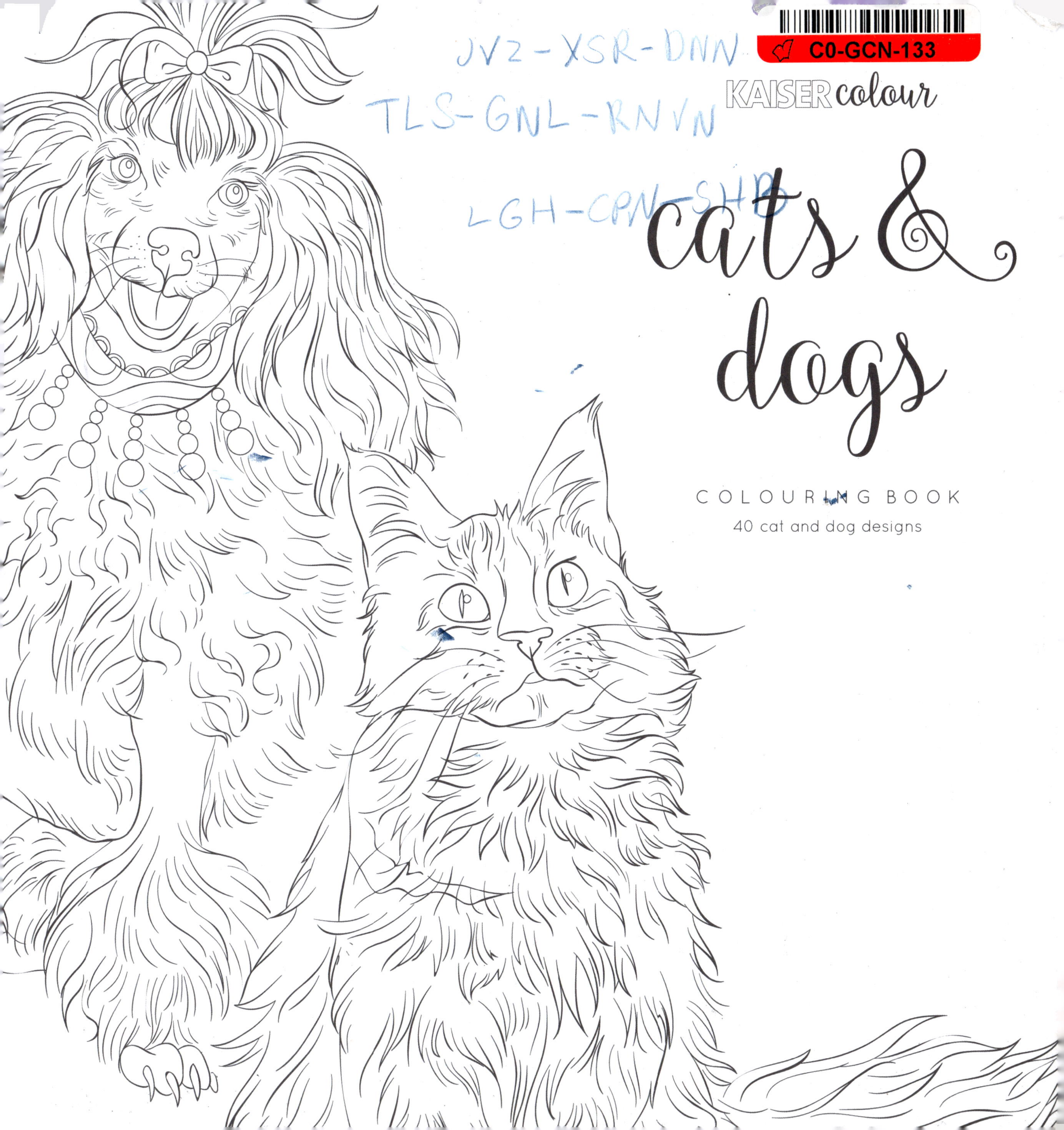

KAISERCRAFT

Kaisercraft Pty Ltd.
2 Bayldon Crt, Breakwater
3219, Victoria
Australia
www.kaisercraft.com.au
www.luckydip.design

First printed in May 2016

ISBN: 978 - 1 - 925405 - 39 - 2

Proudly Printed in Australia

All illustrations featured in the book are original.

MIX
Paper from responsible sources
FSC® C010983
FSC www.fsc.org

THIS BOOK BELONGS TO

Gracelyn Wilson

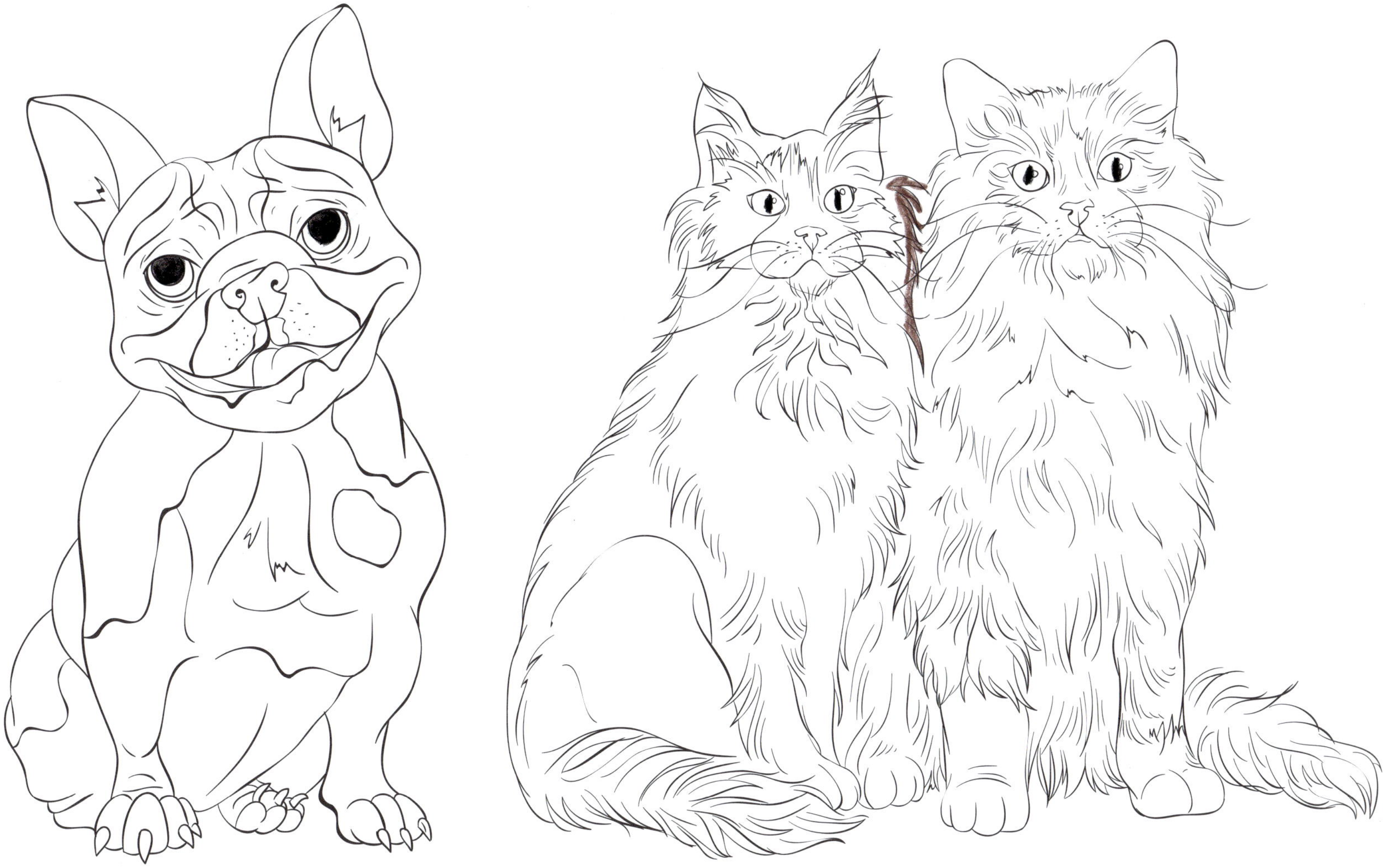

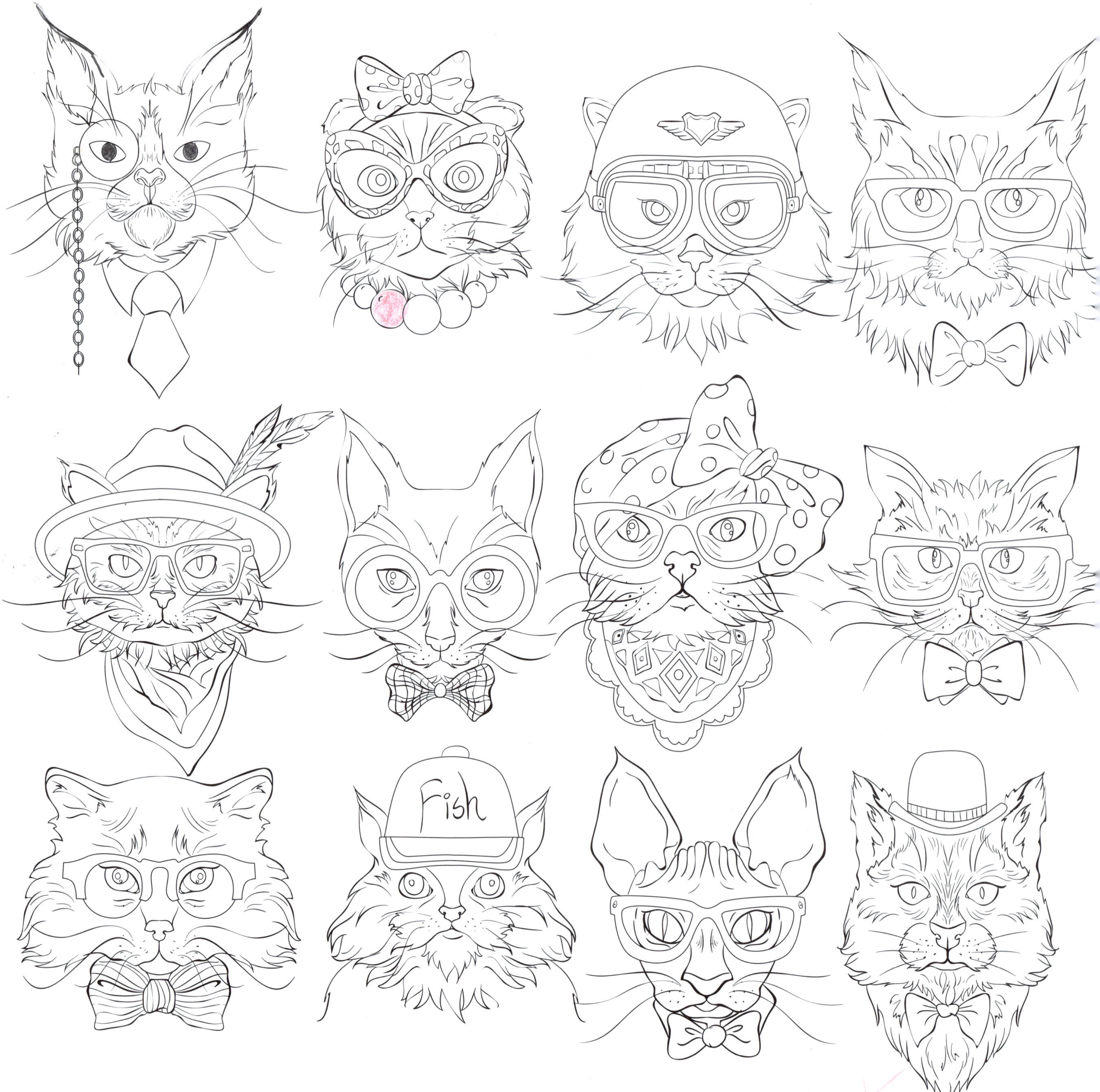
Fish

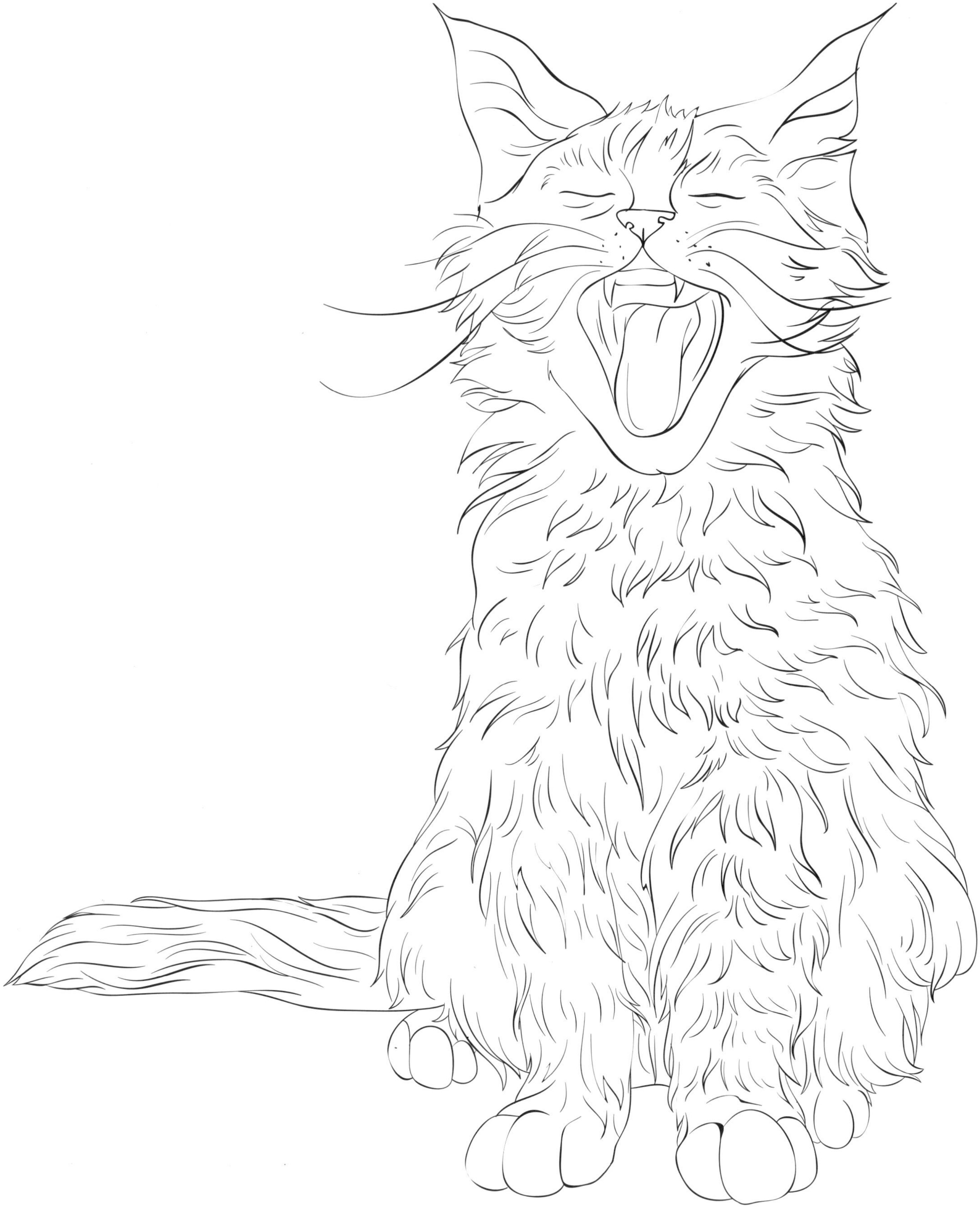

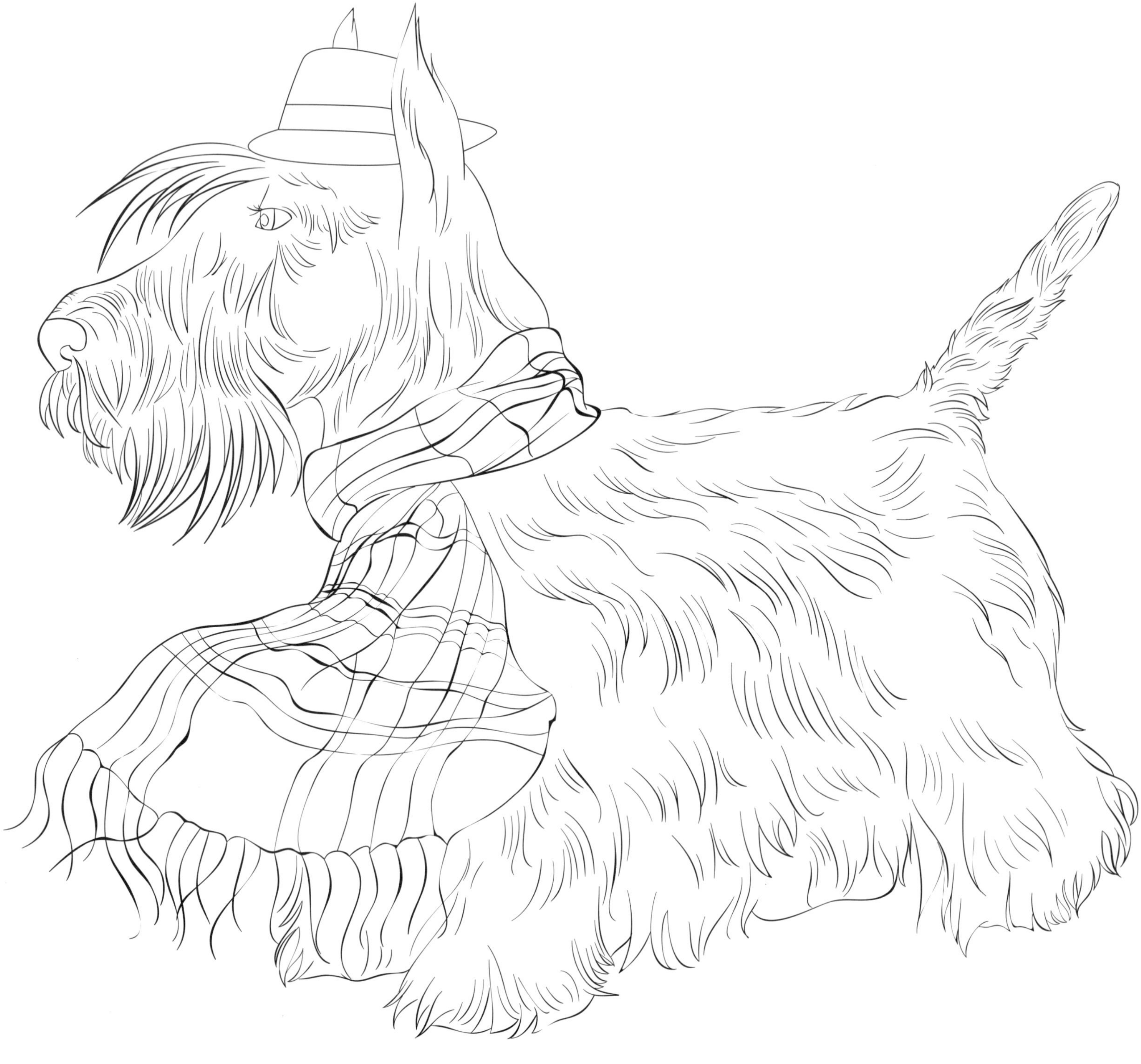

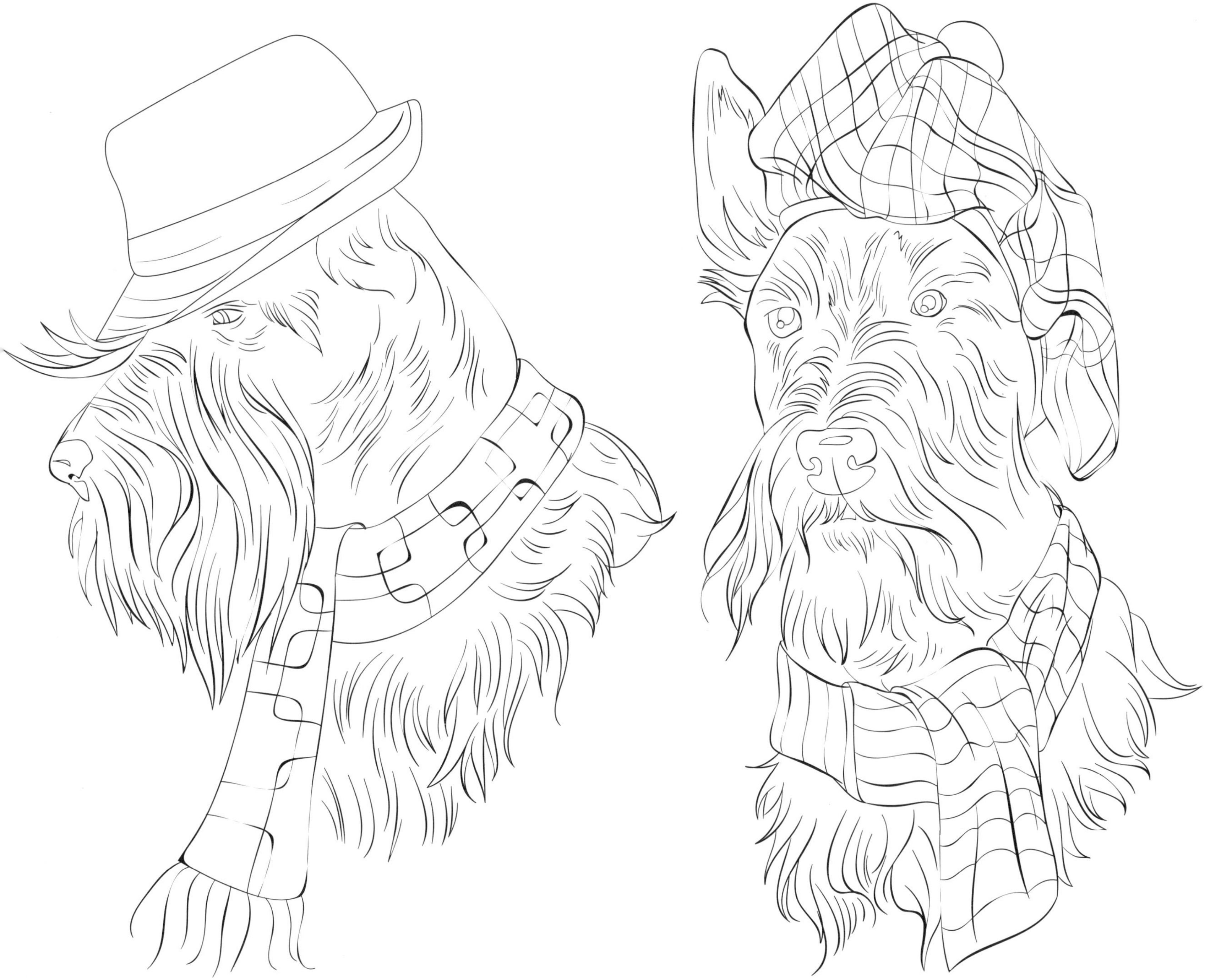

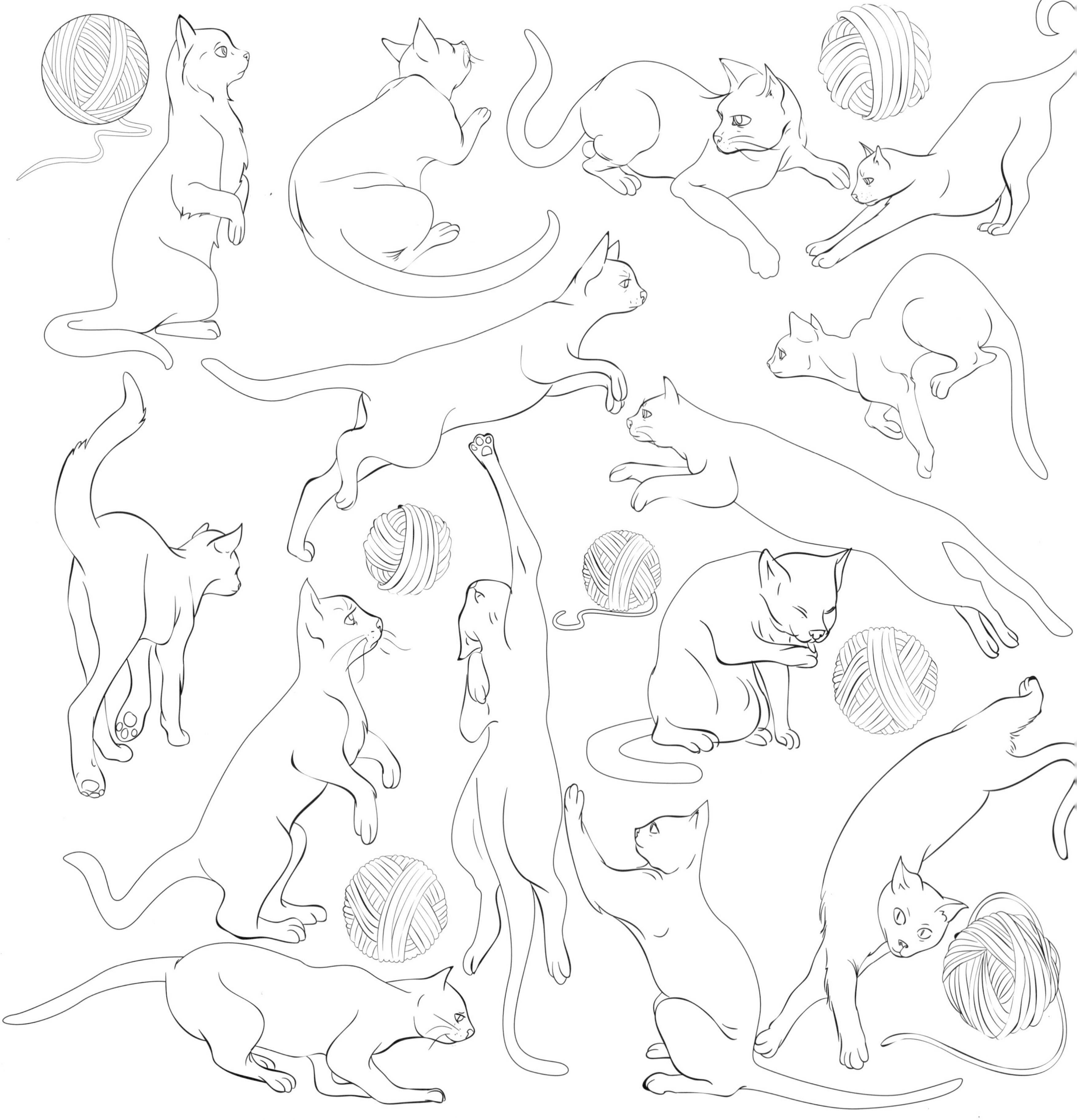

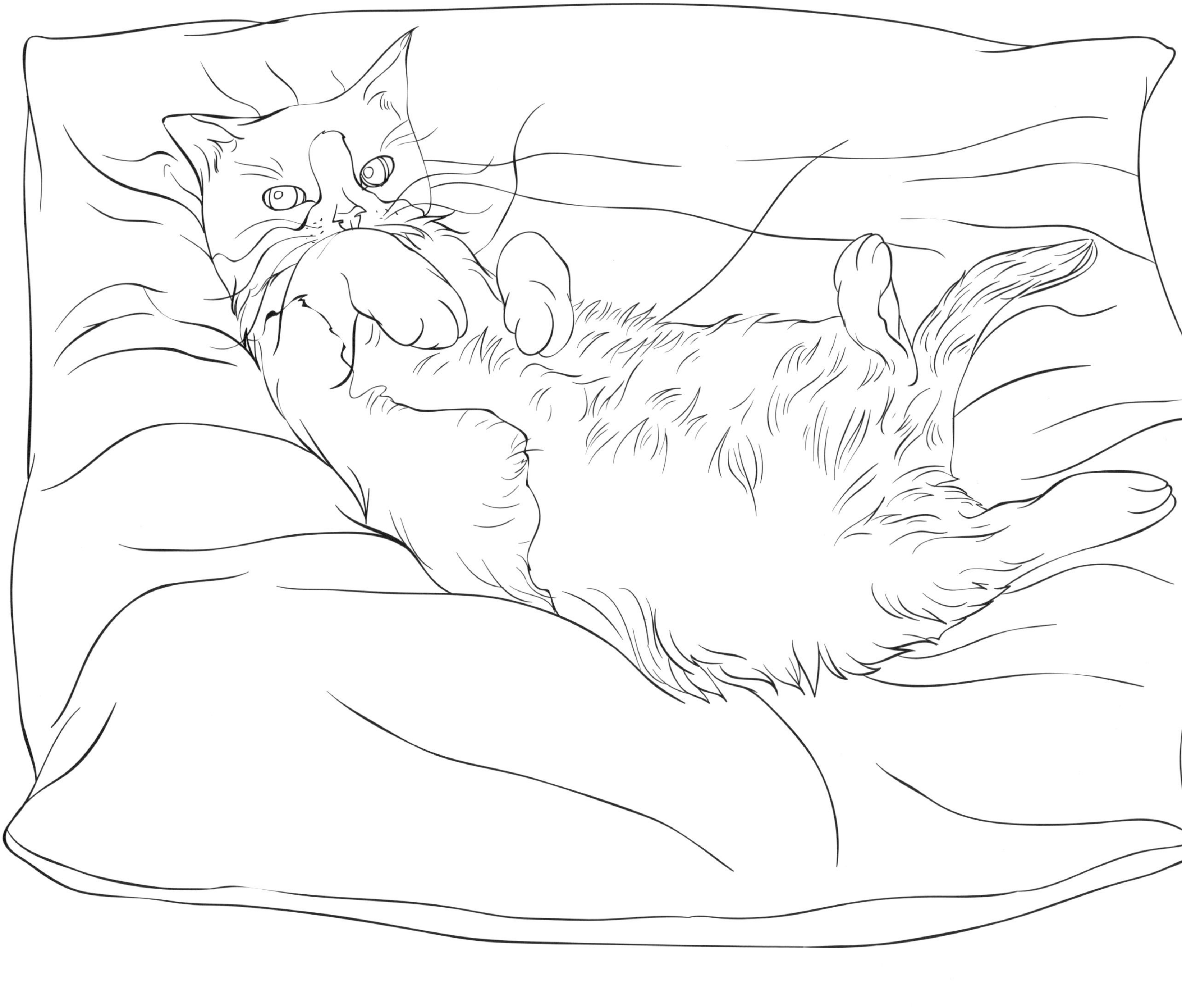

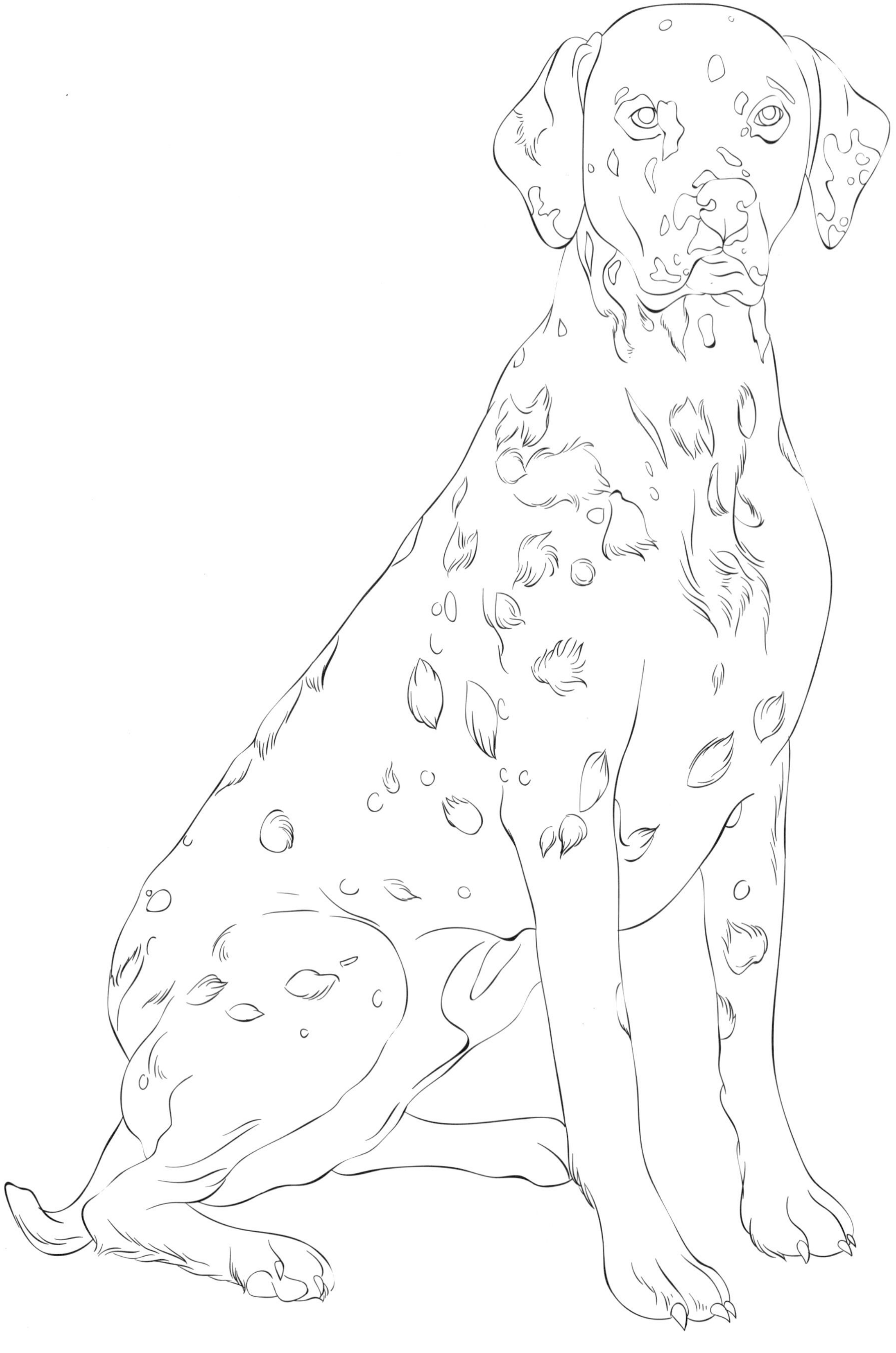

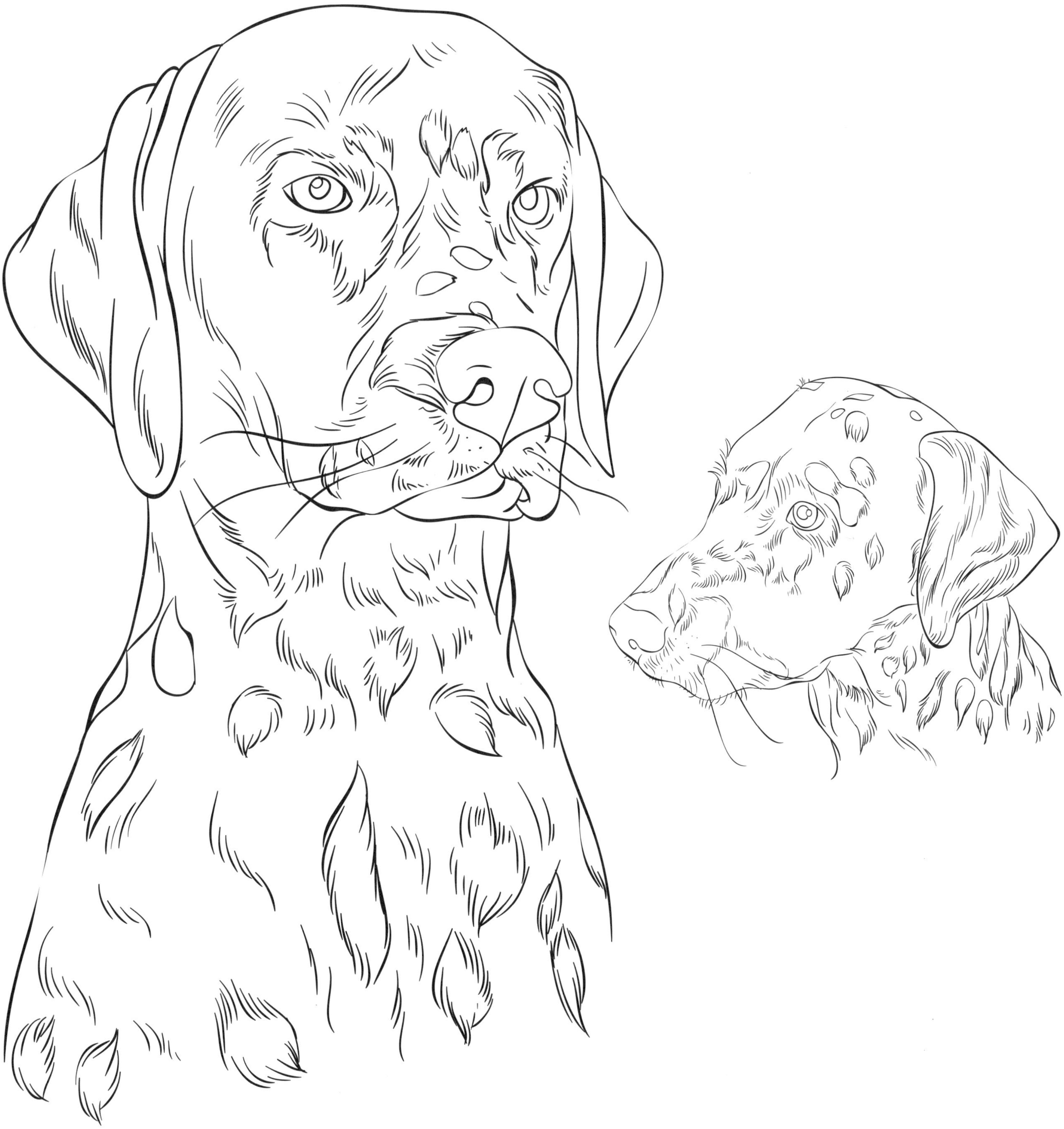

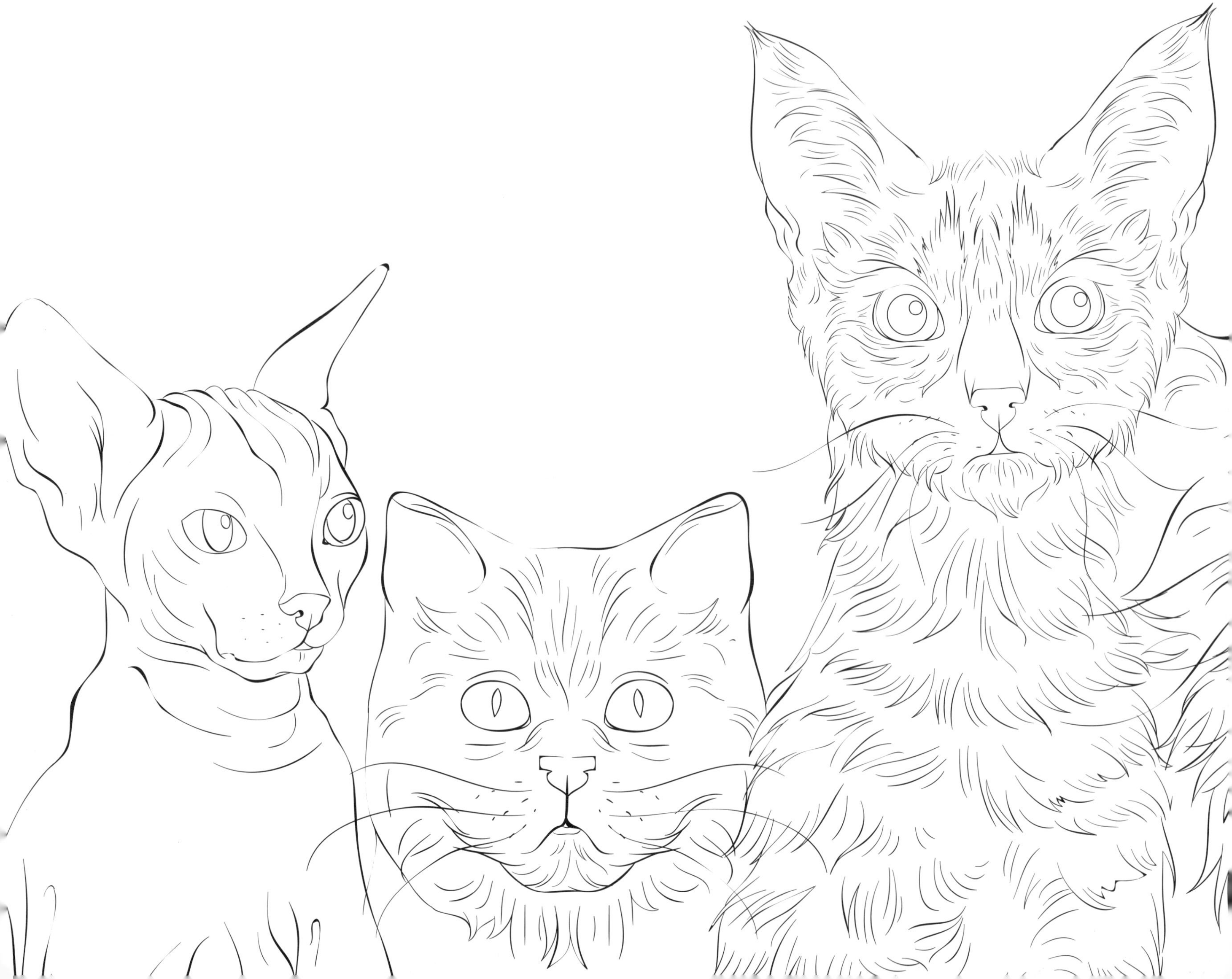

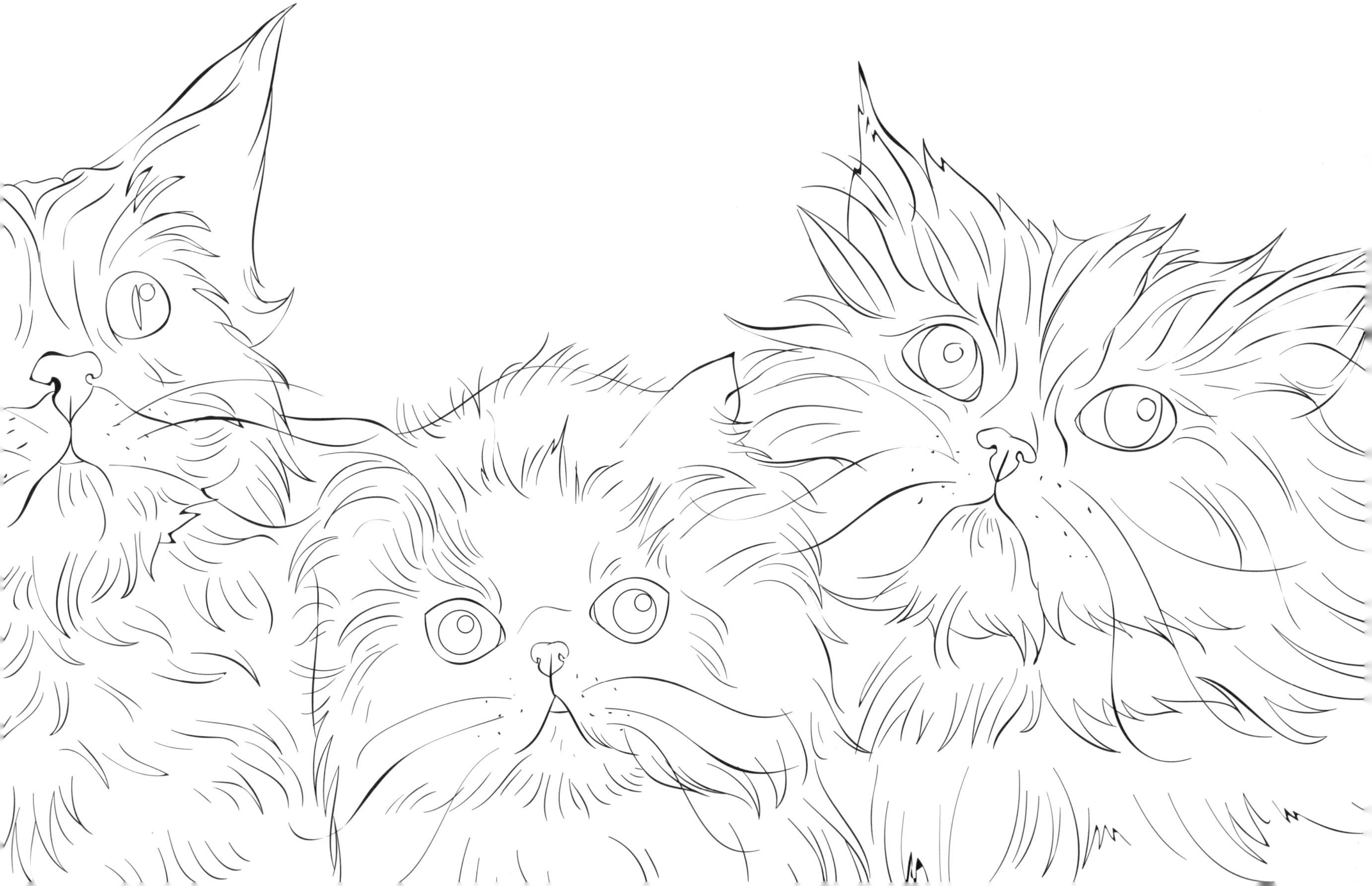

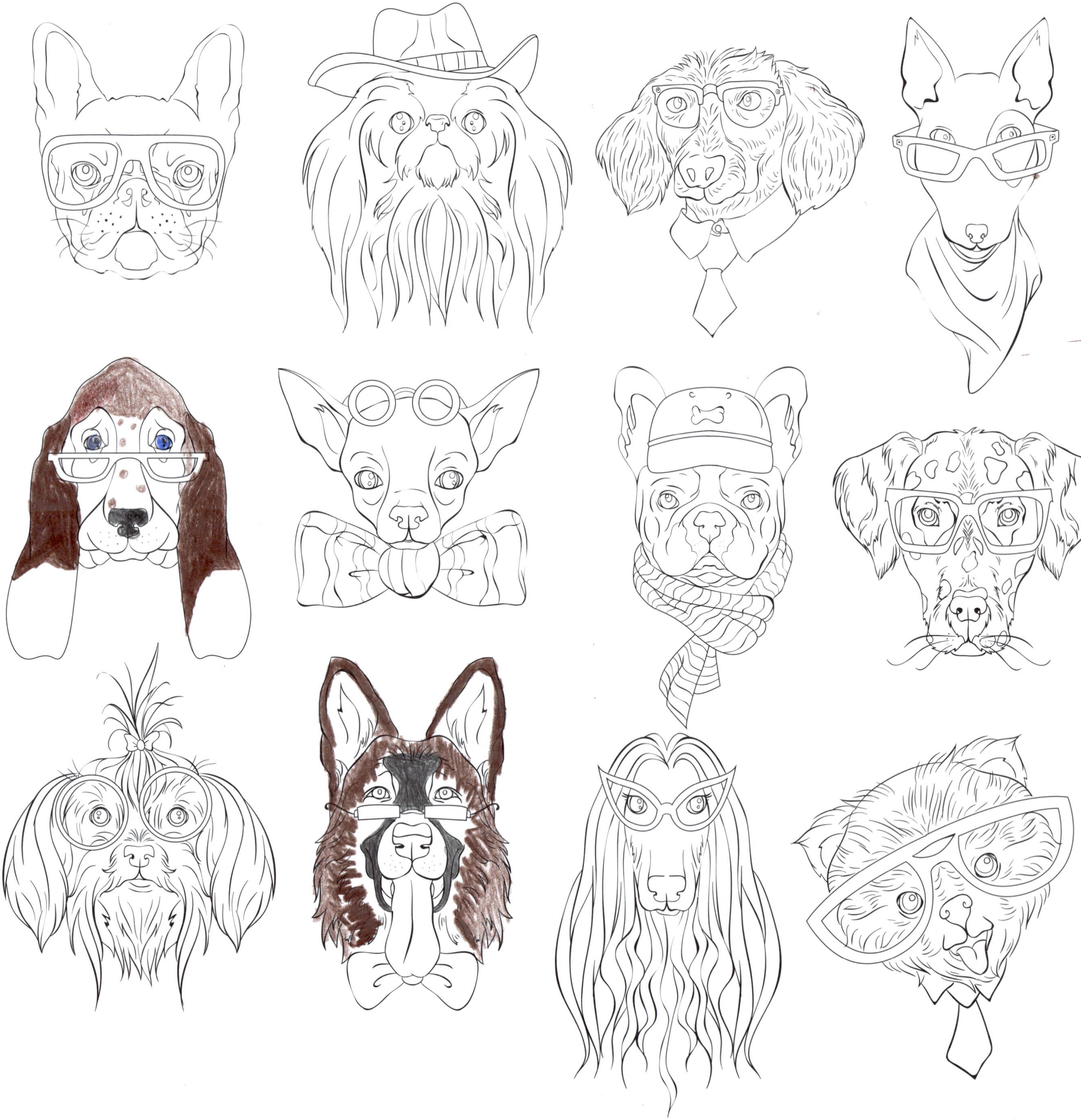

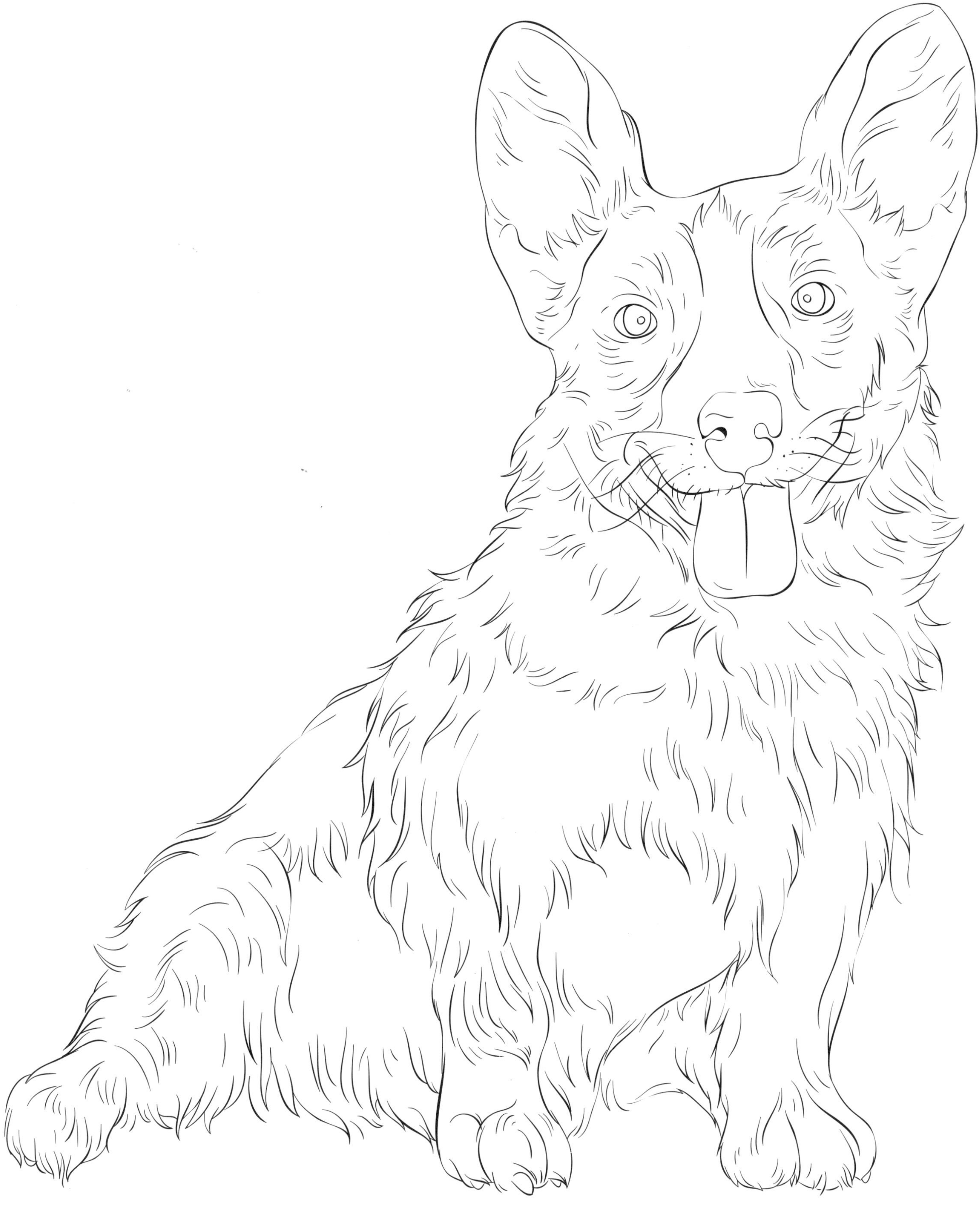

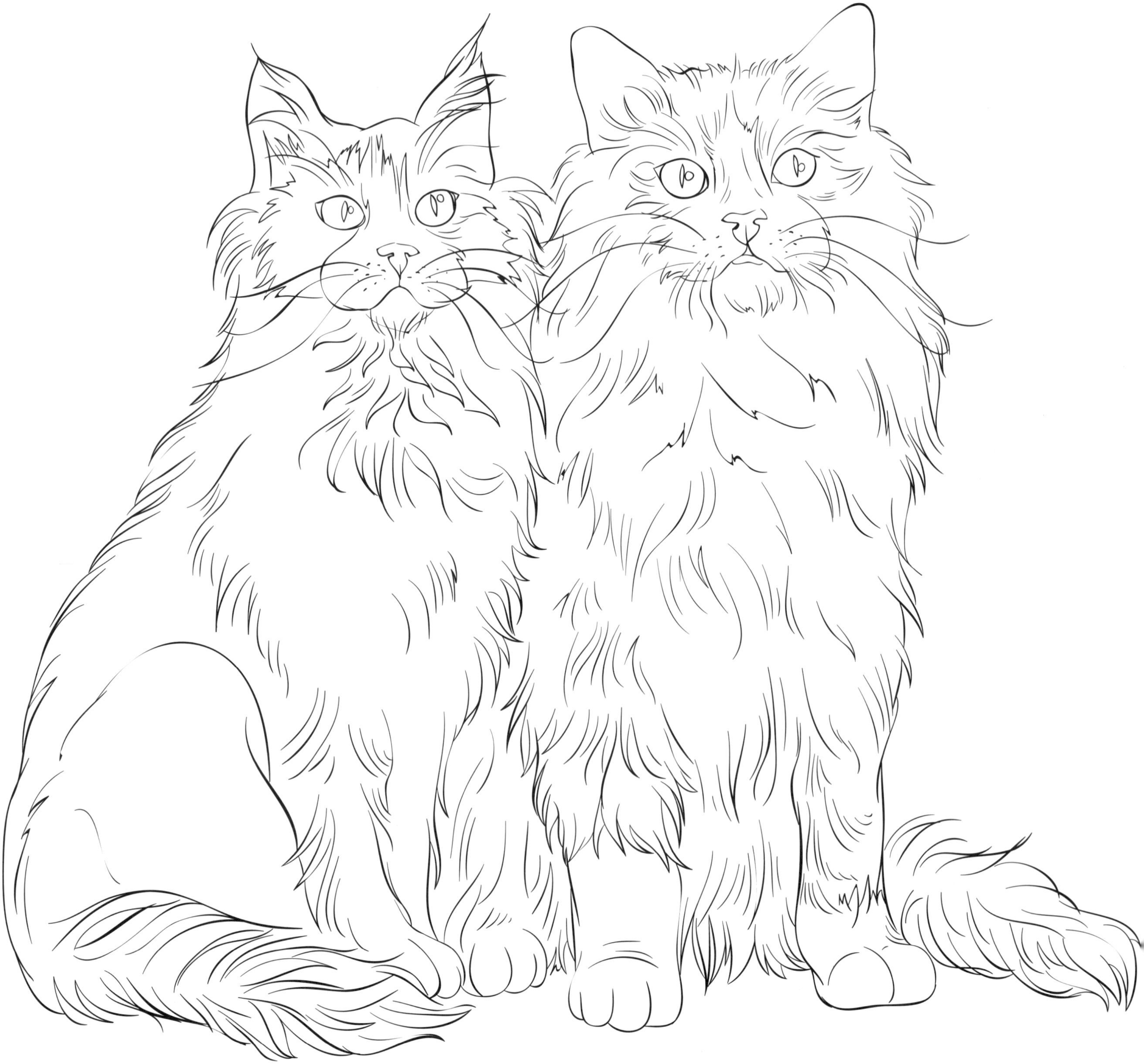

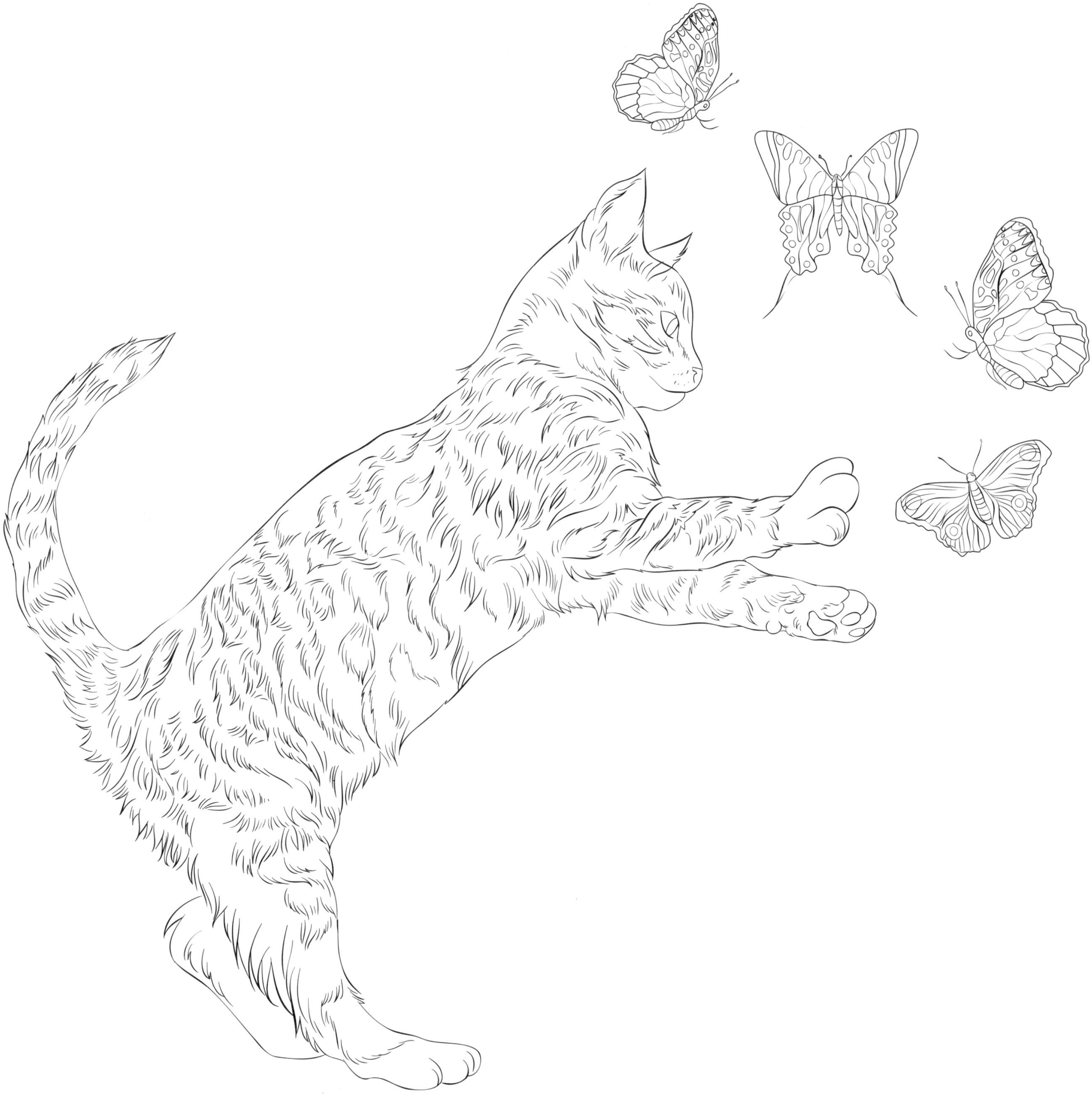

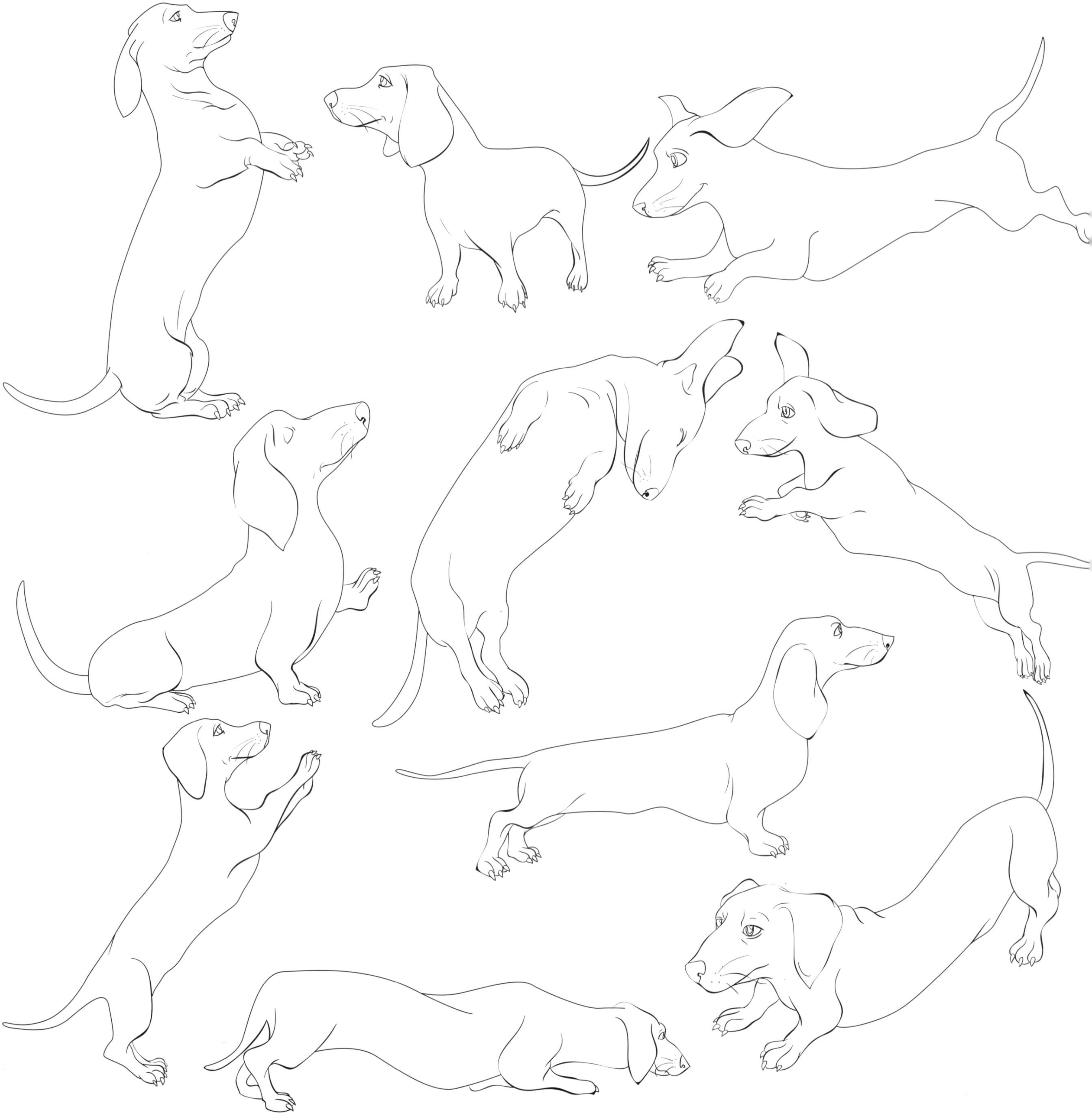

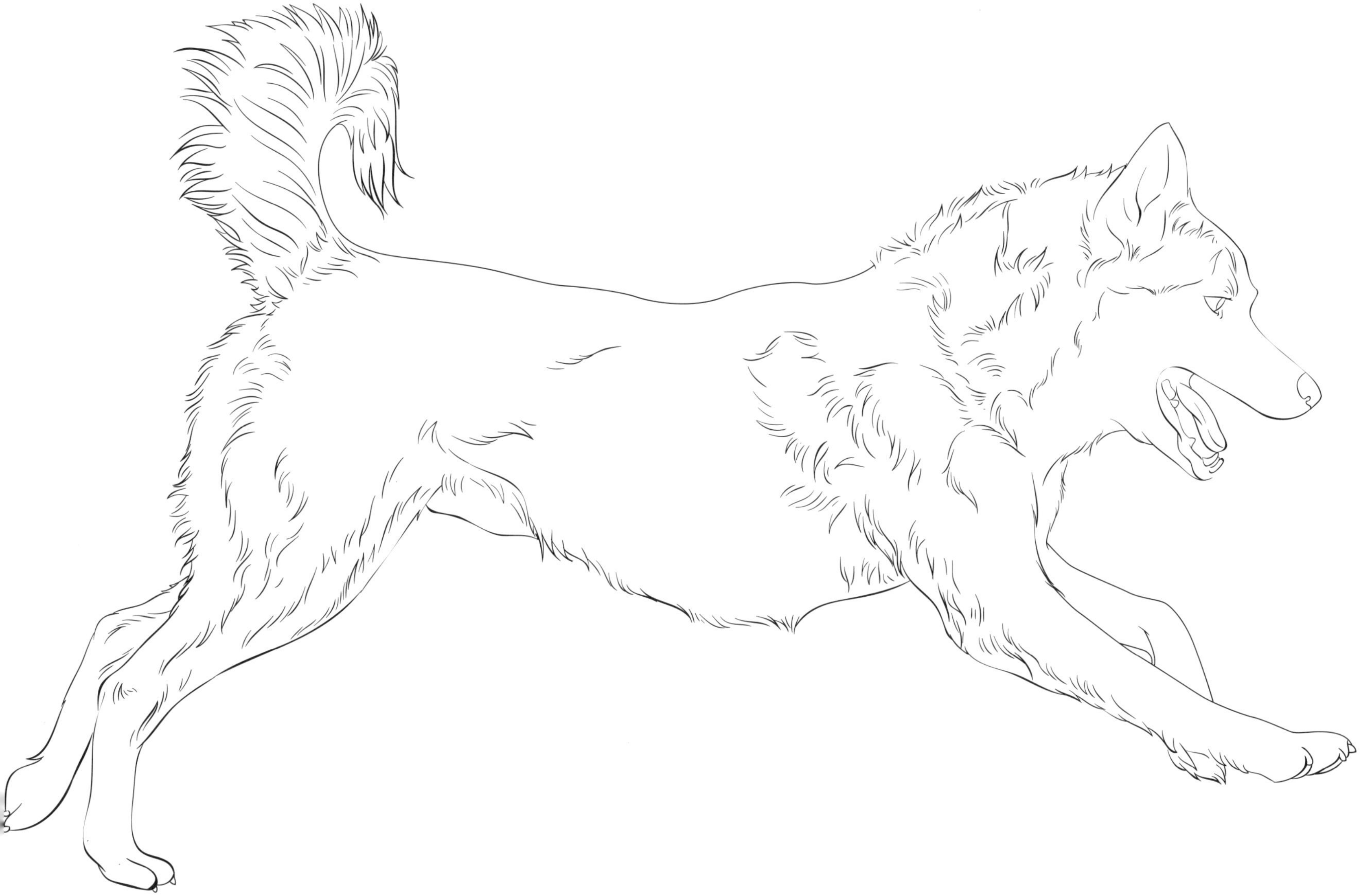

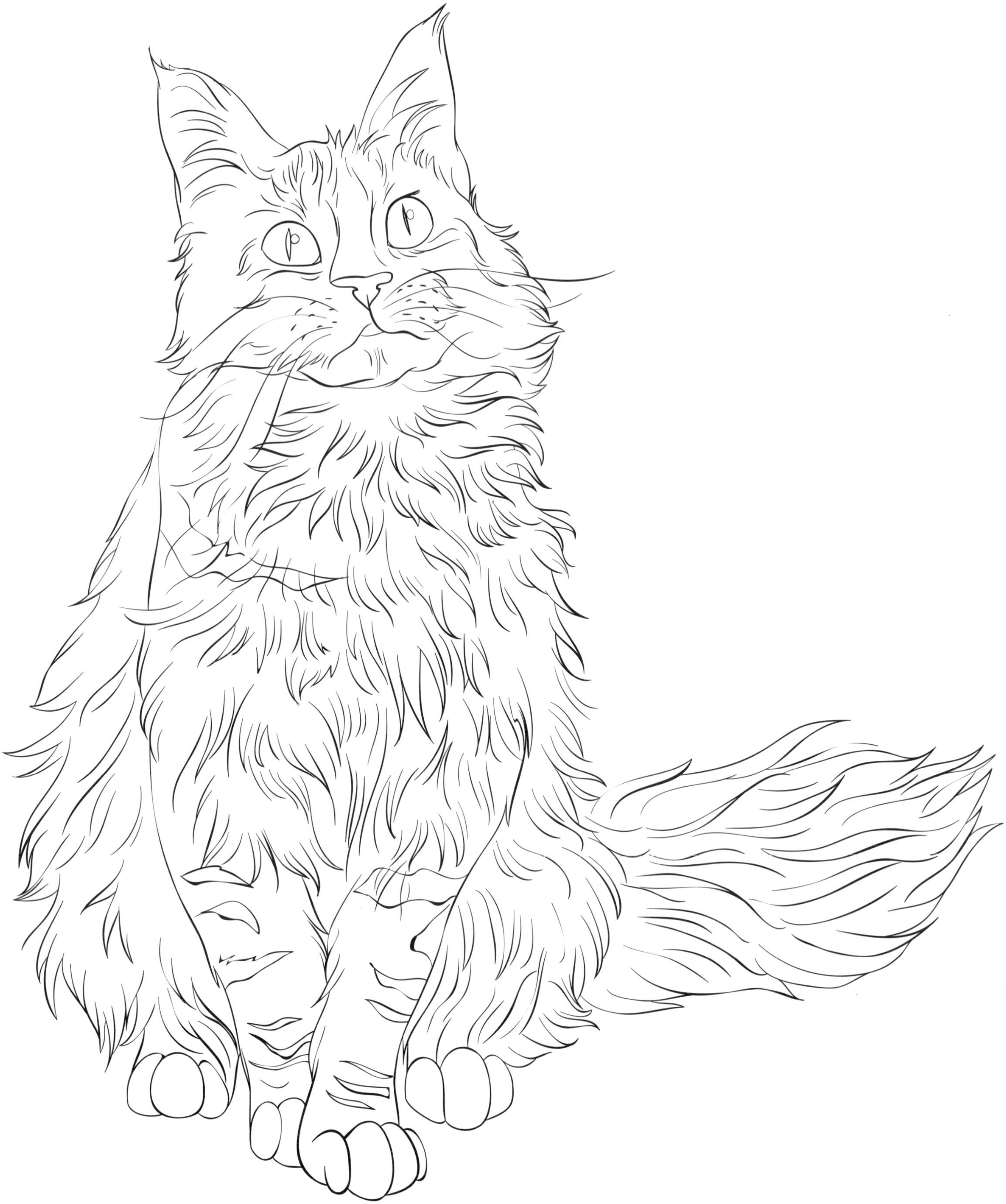

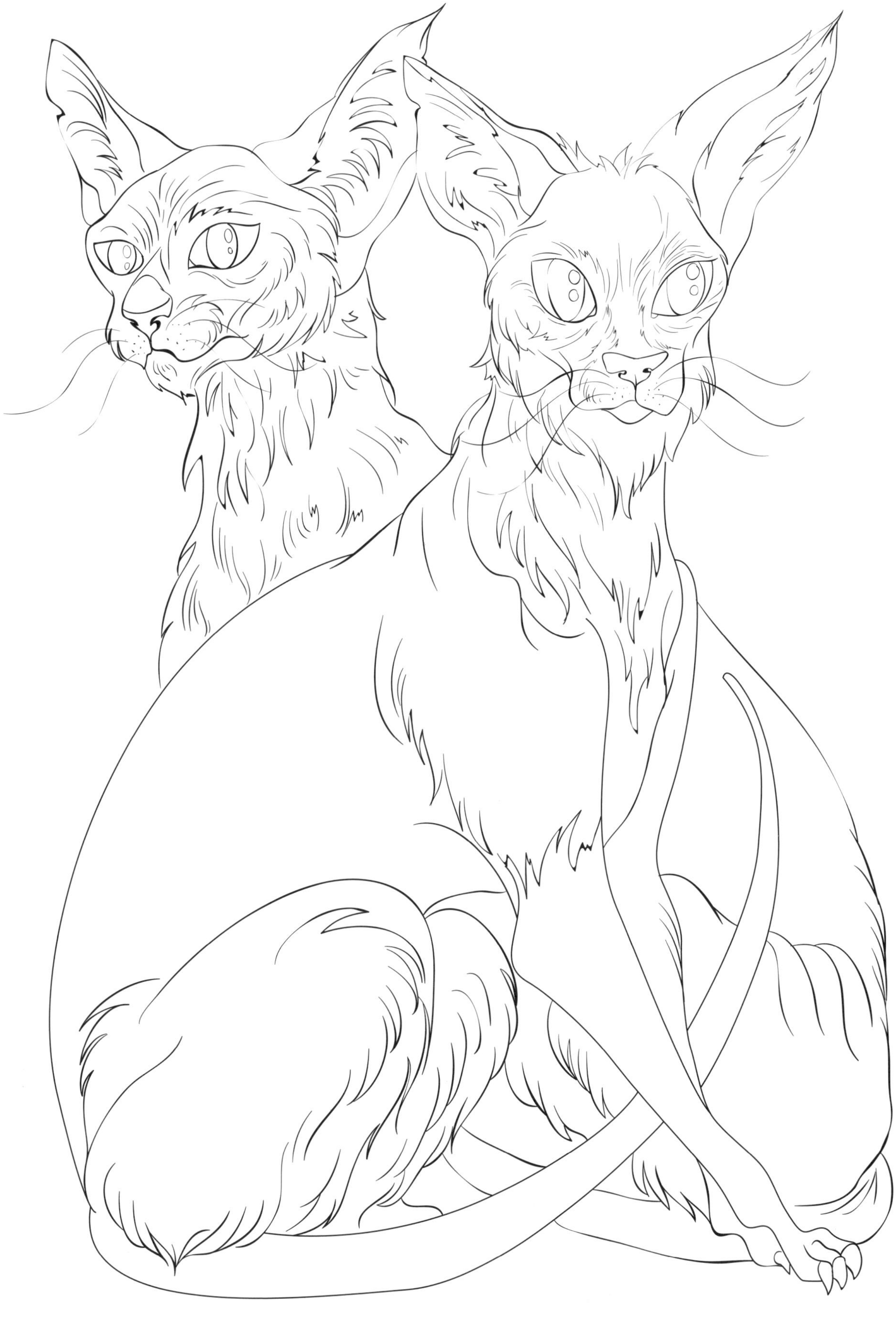

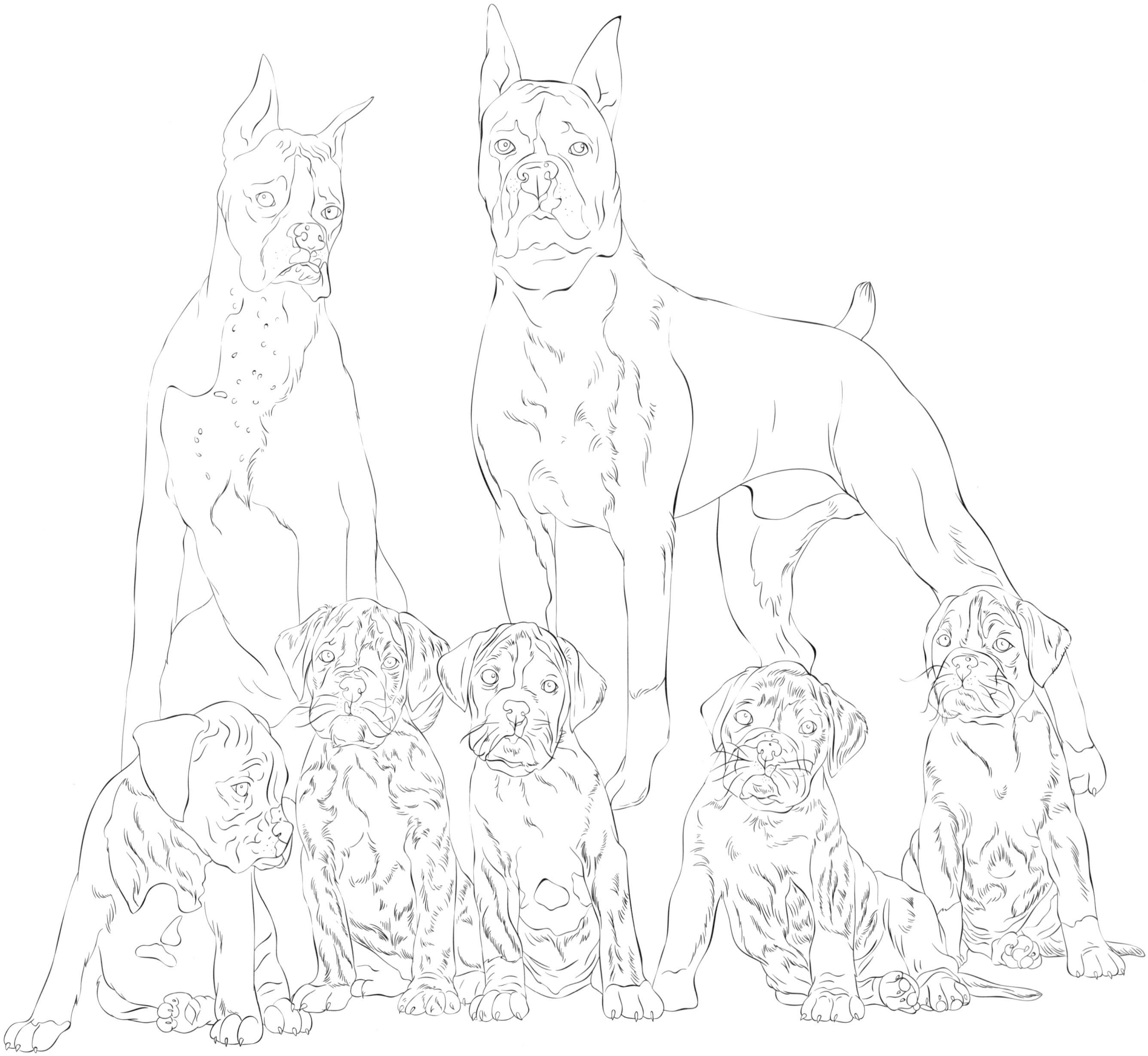

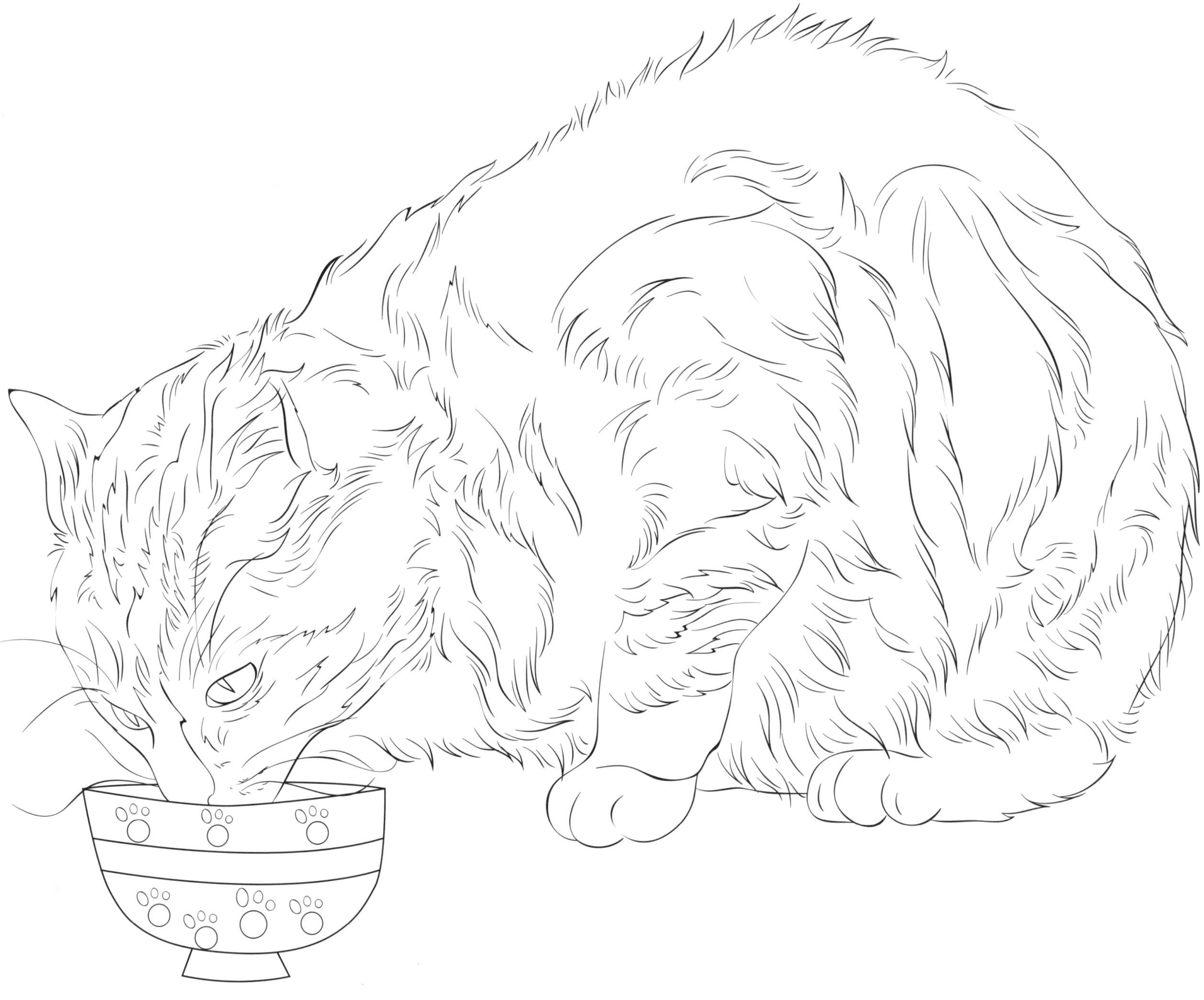

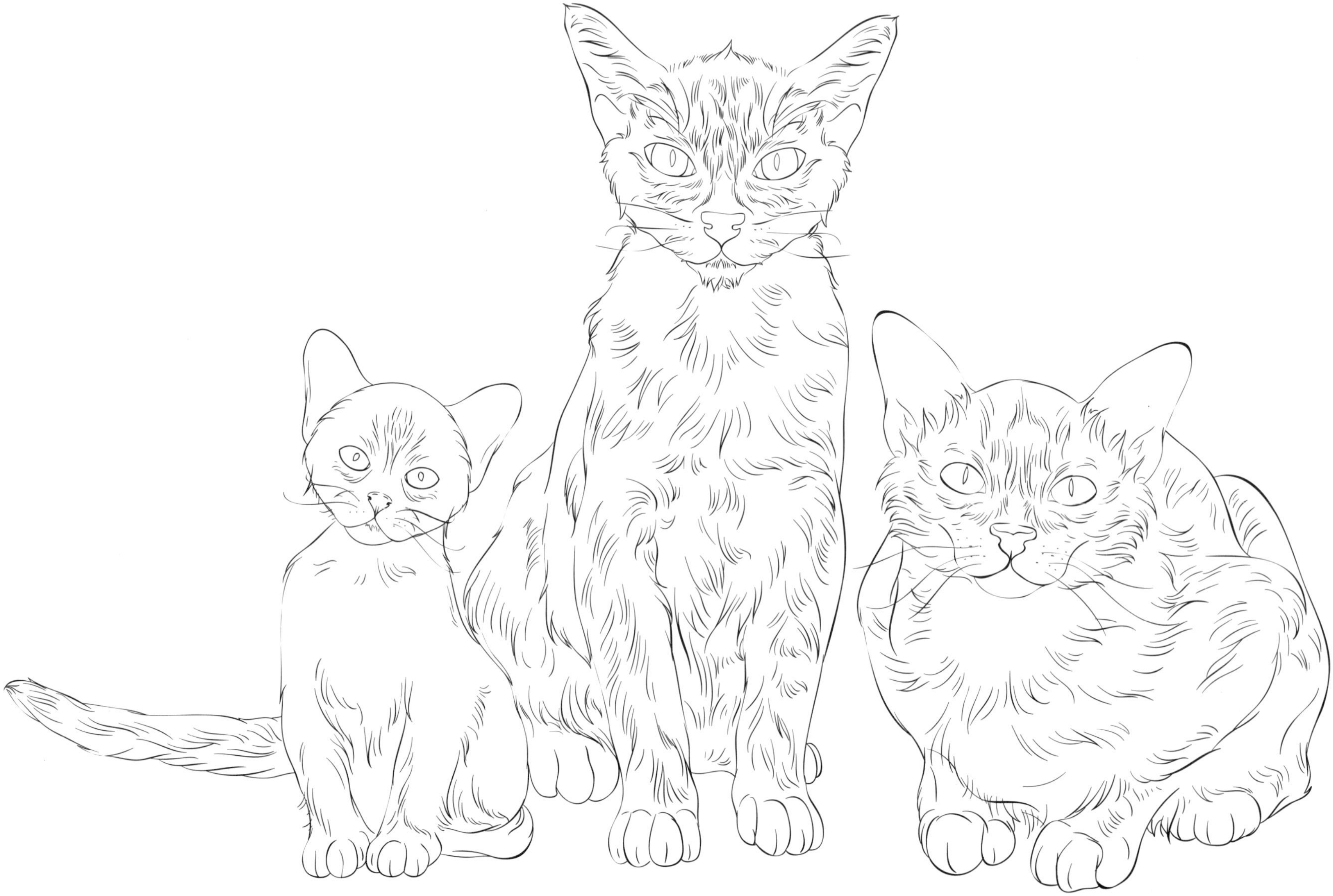

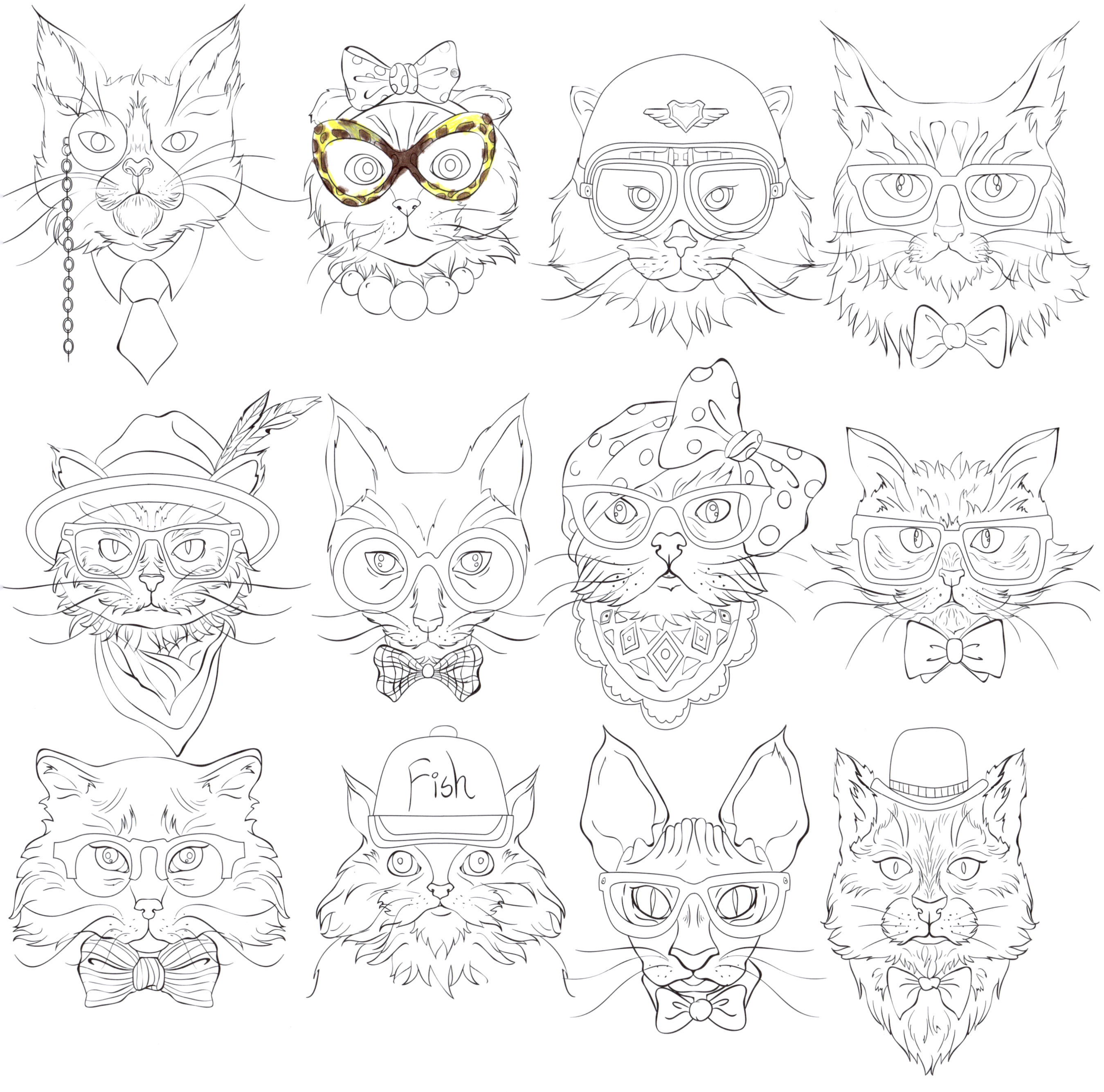
Fish

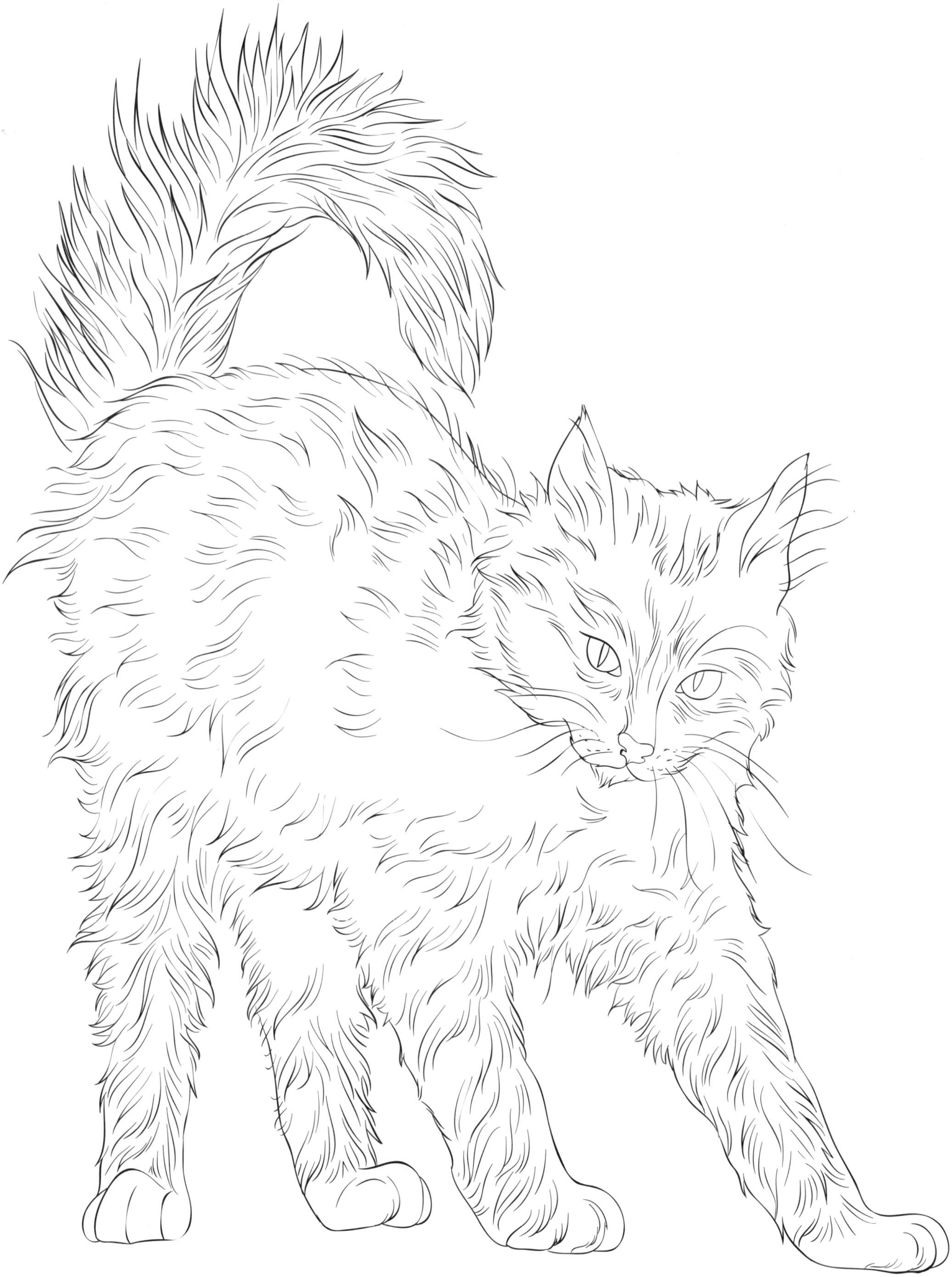

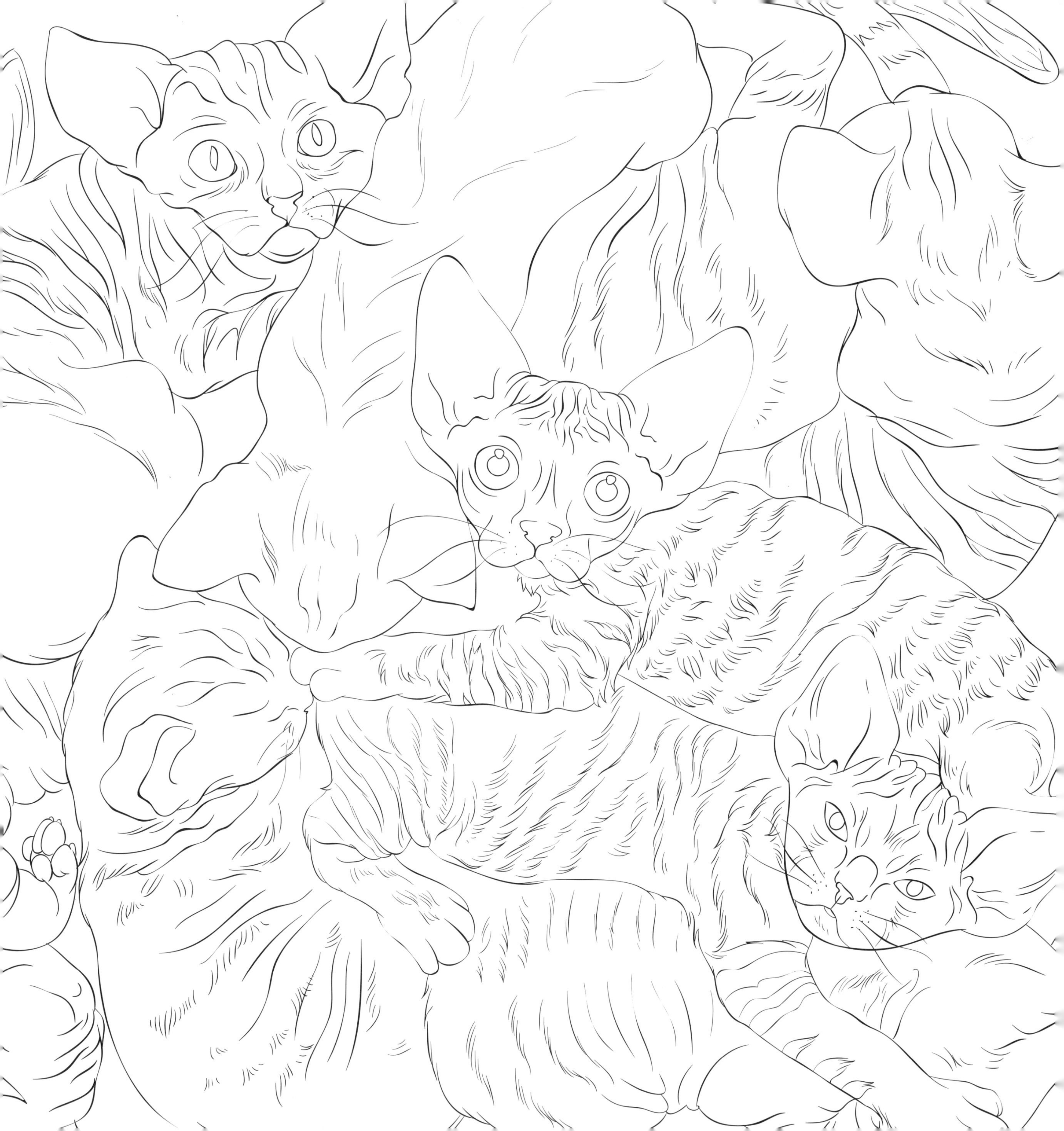

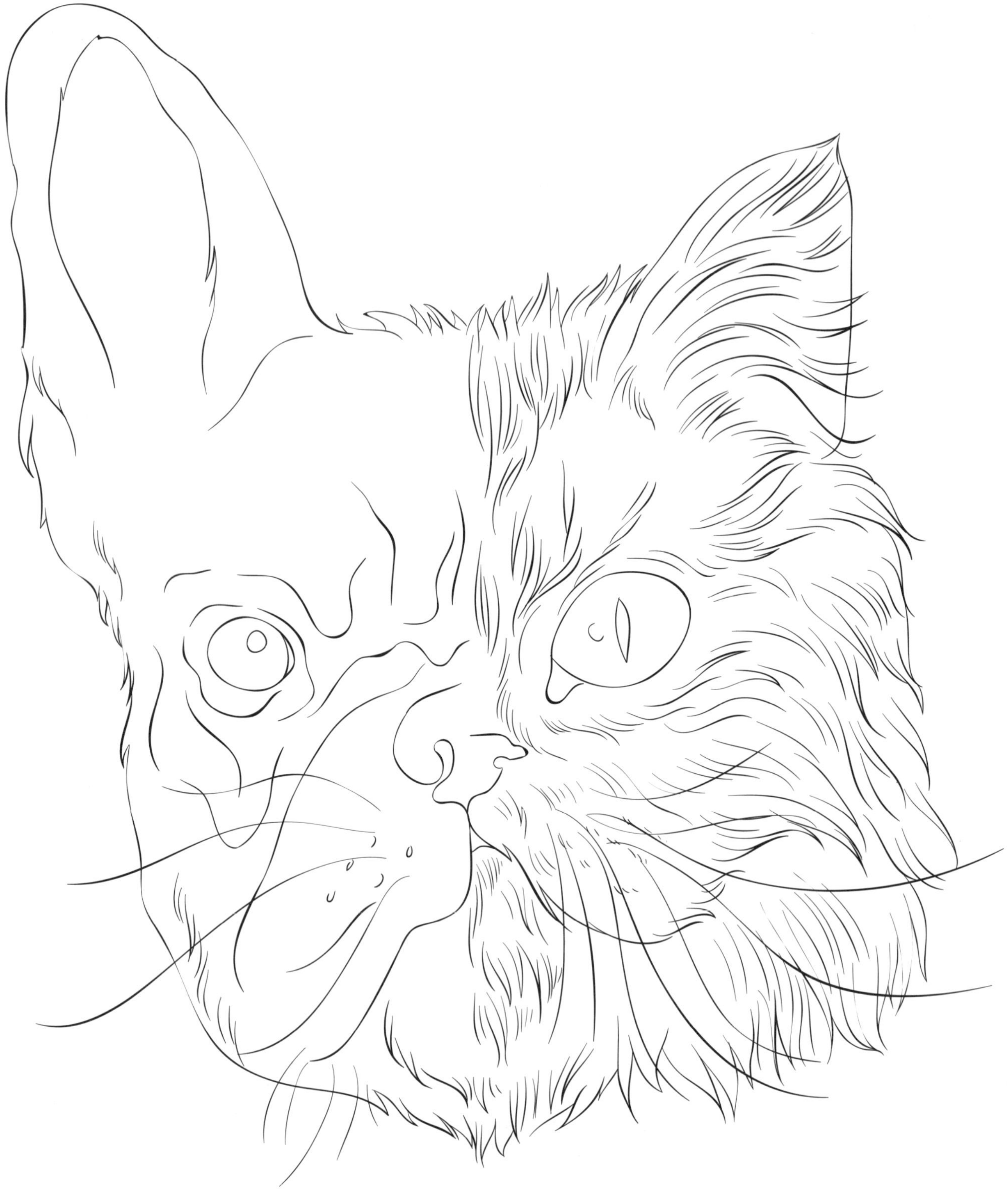

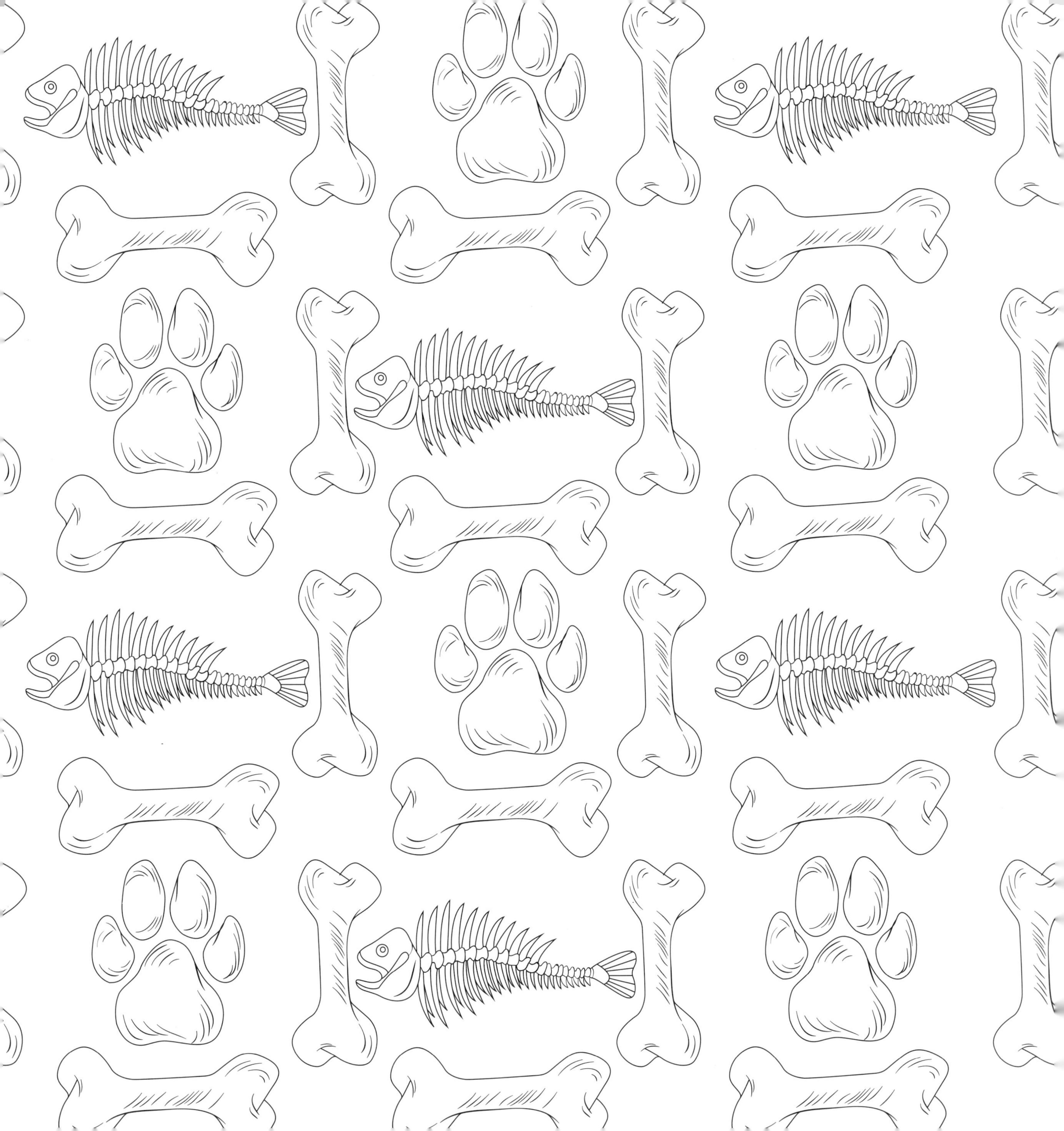

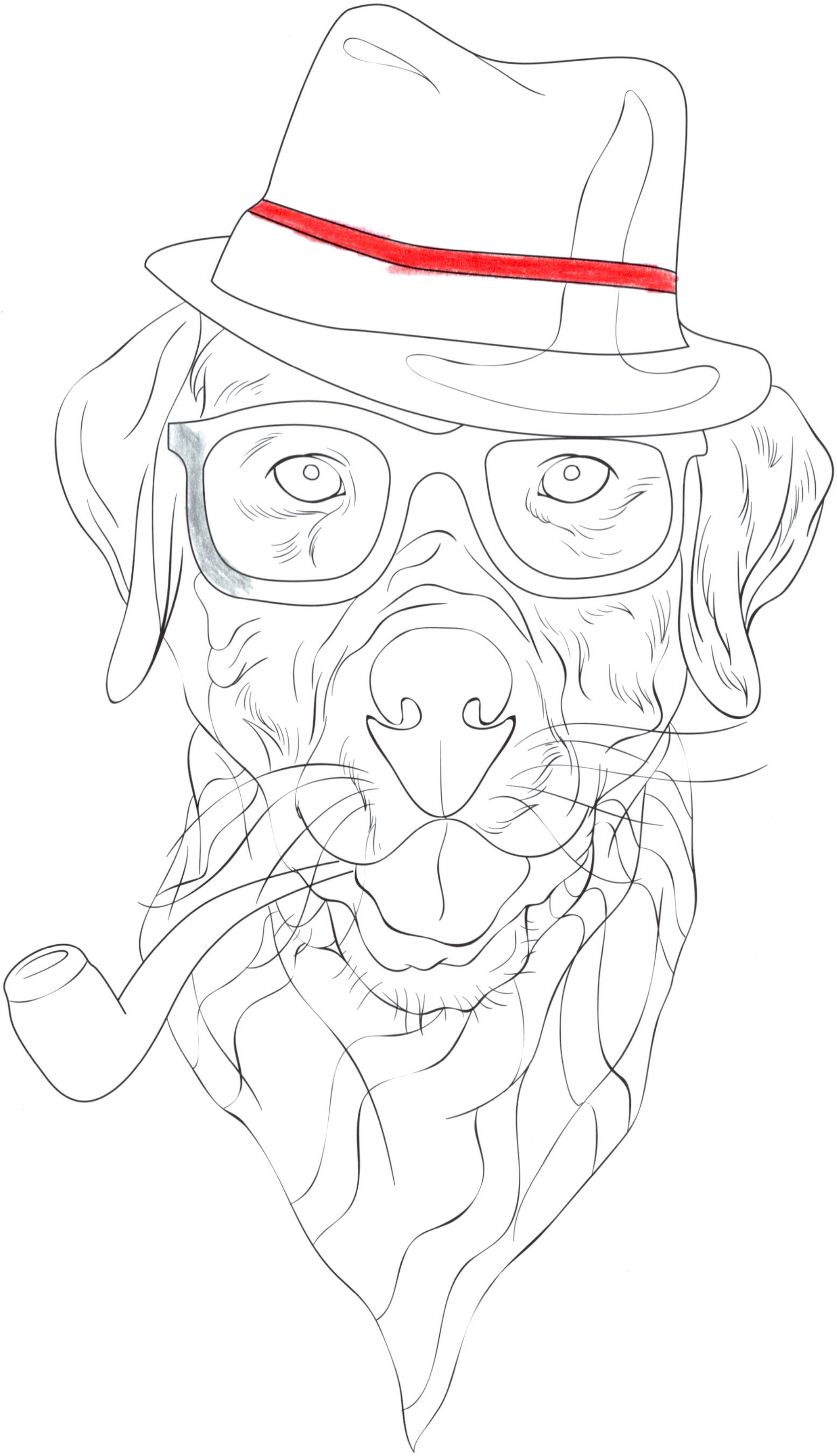

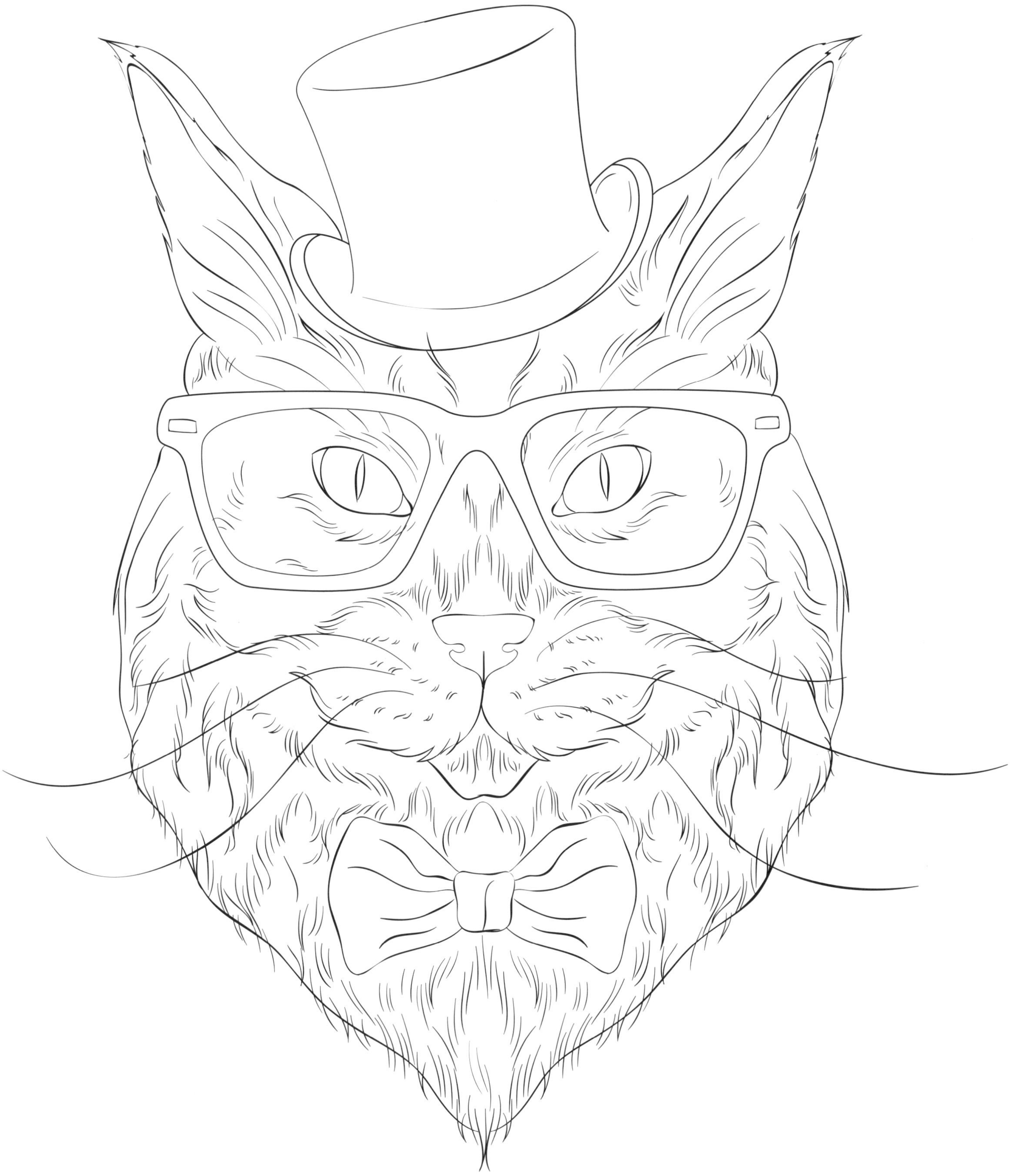

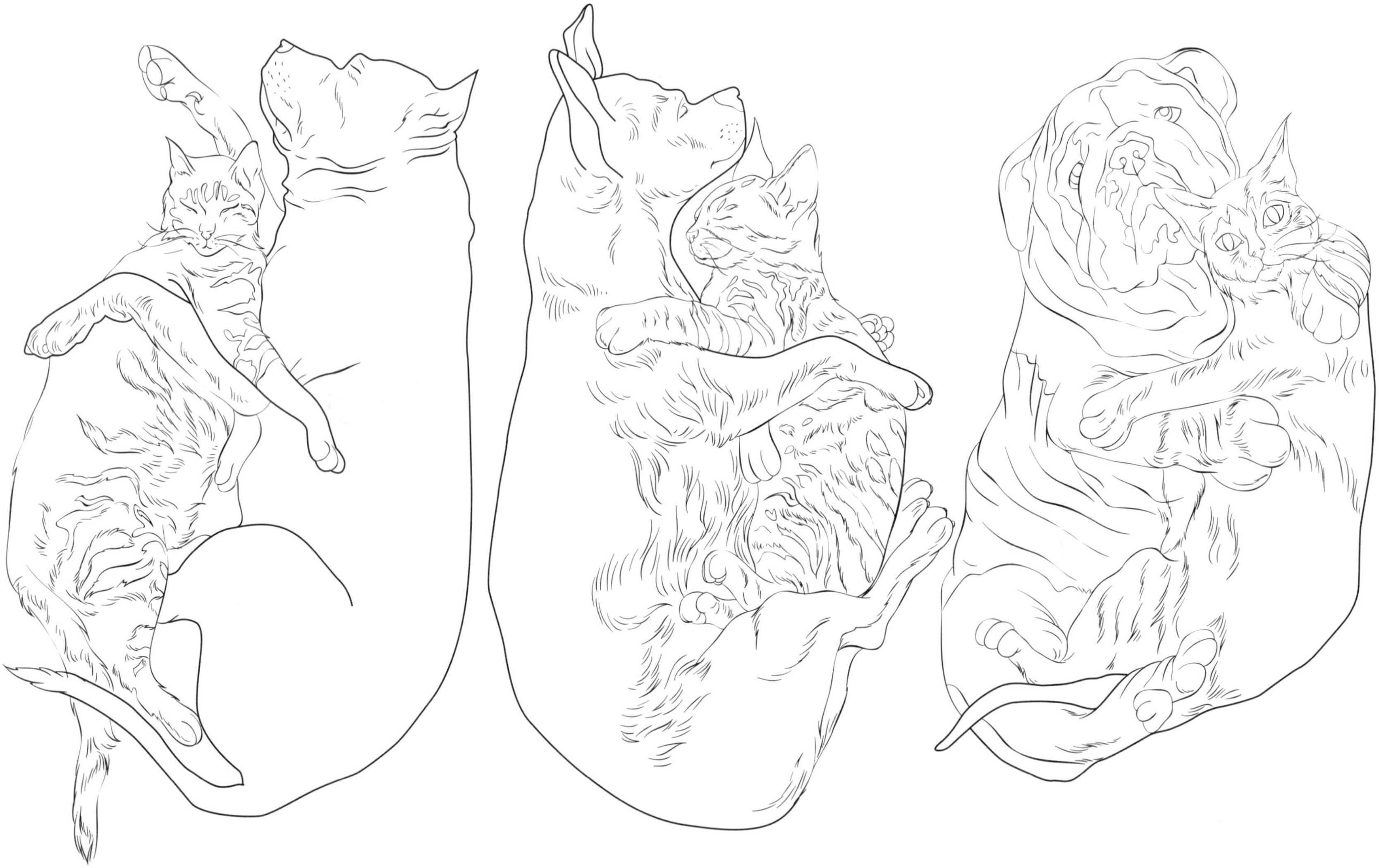

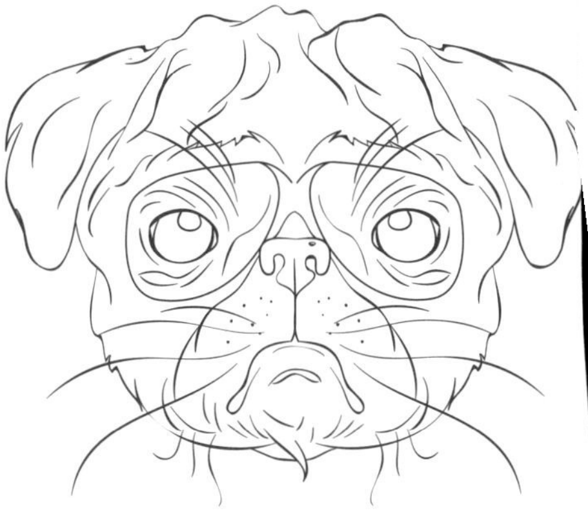
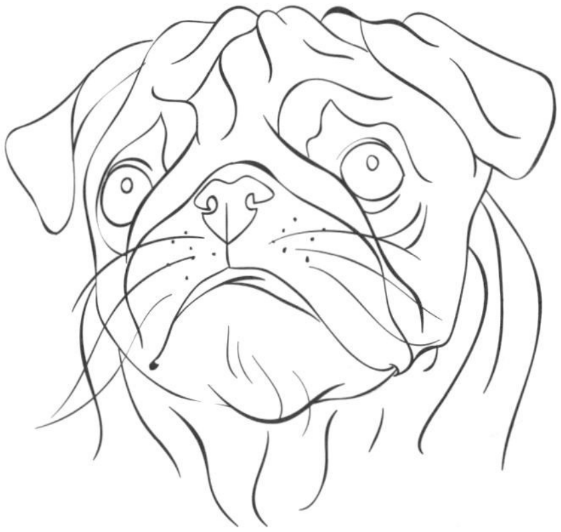
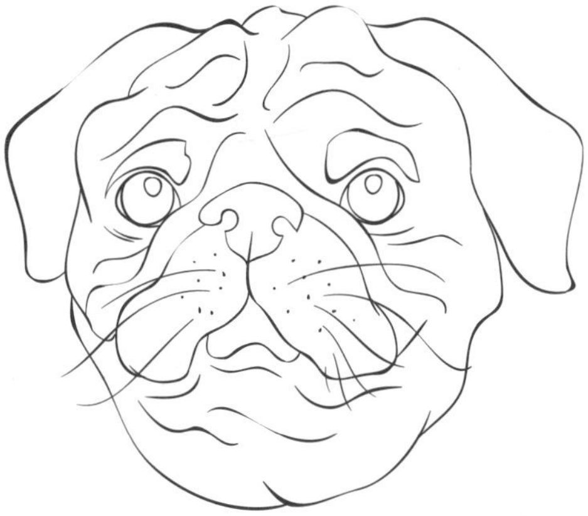
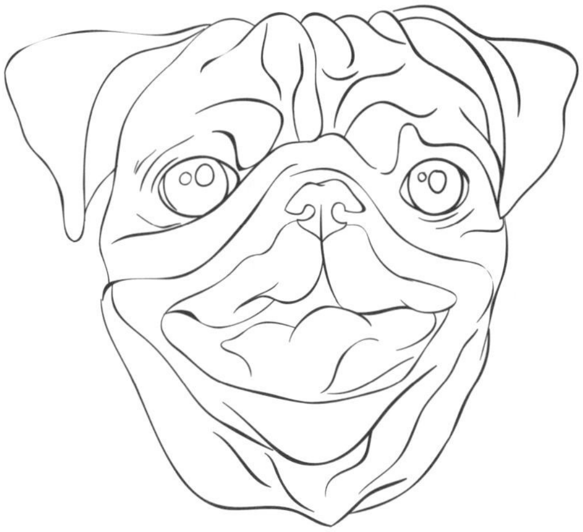
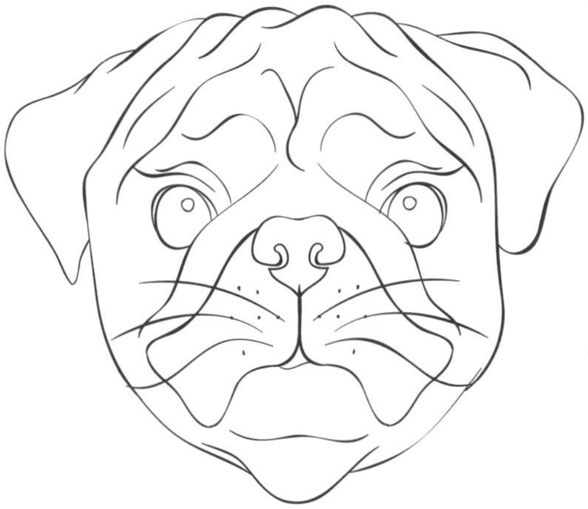
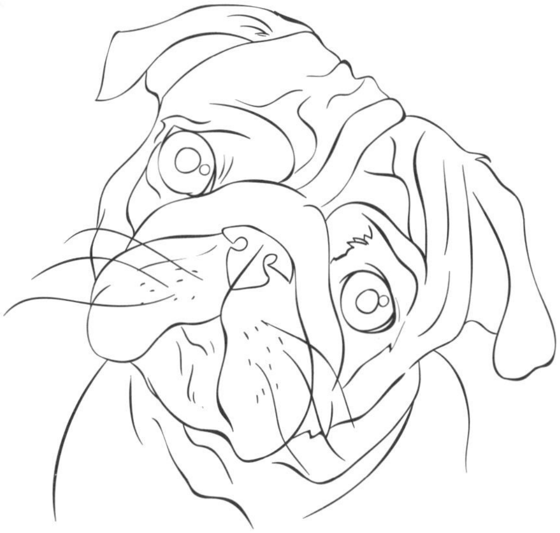
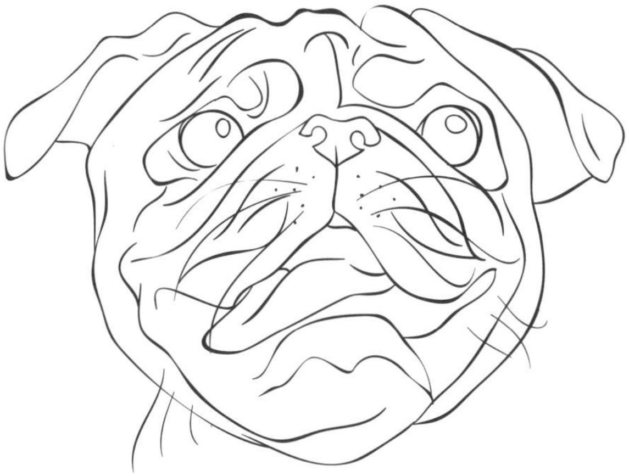

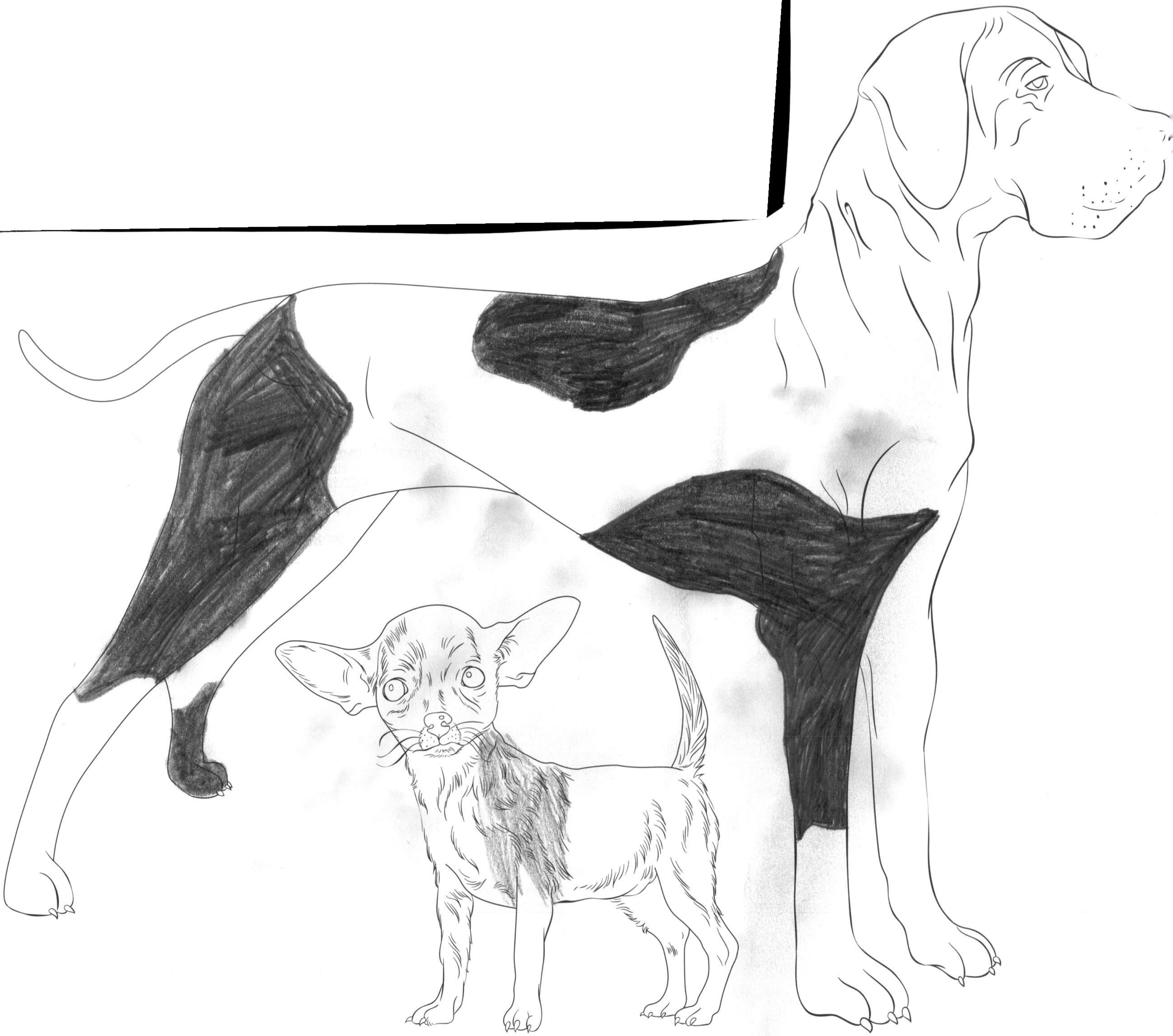

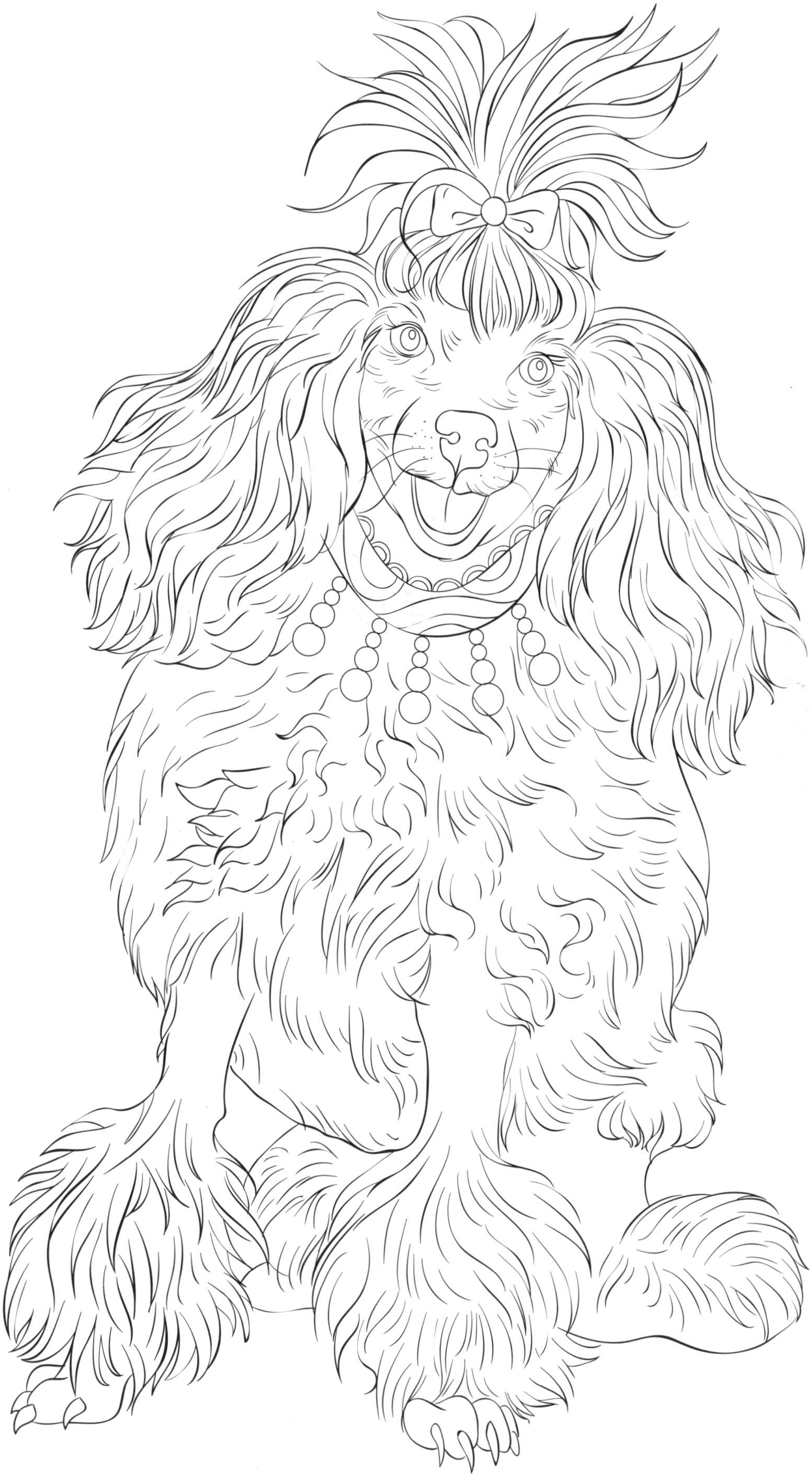

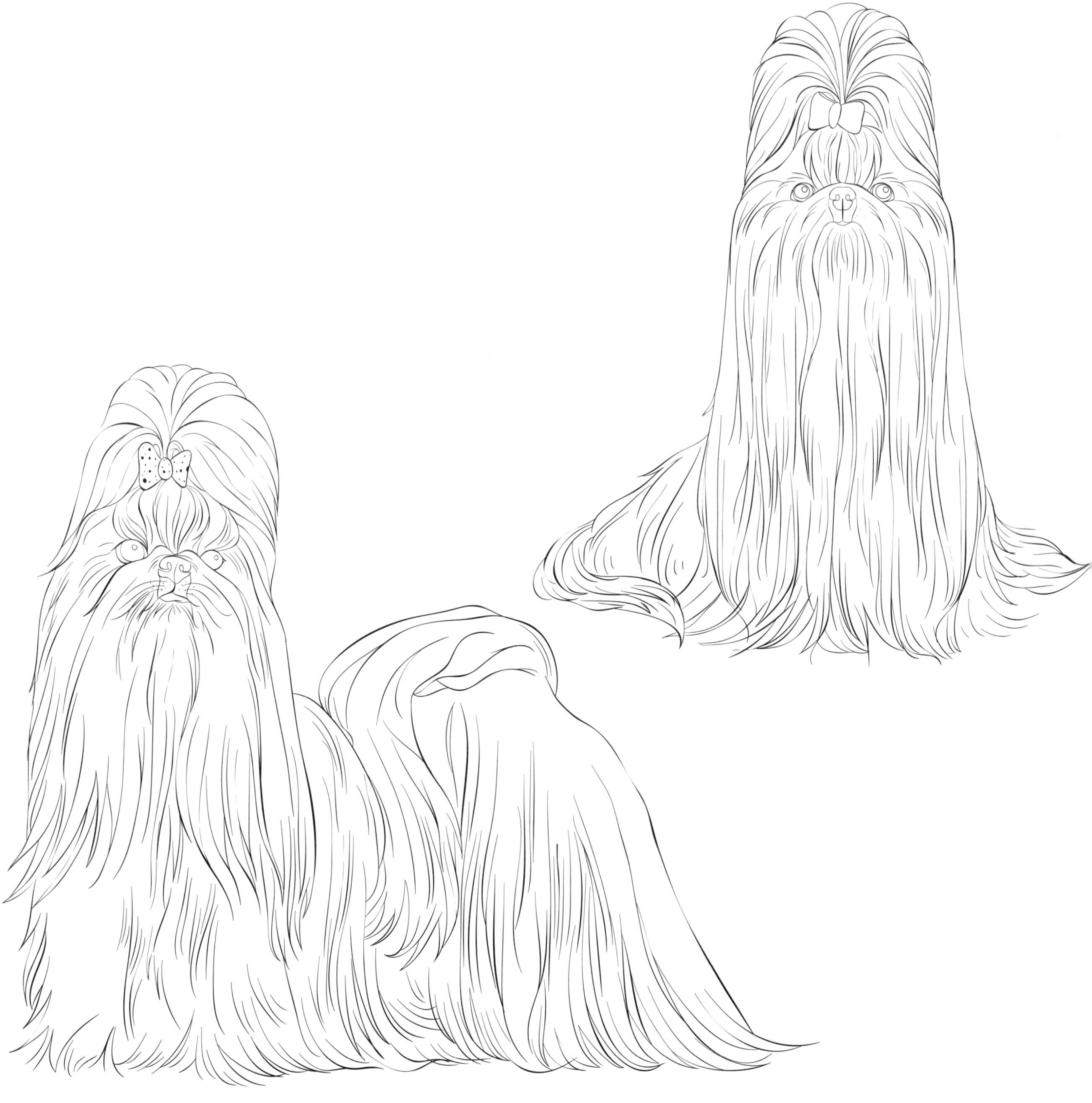

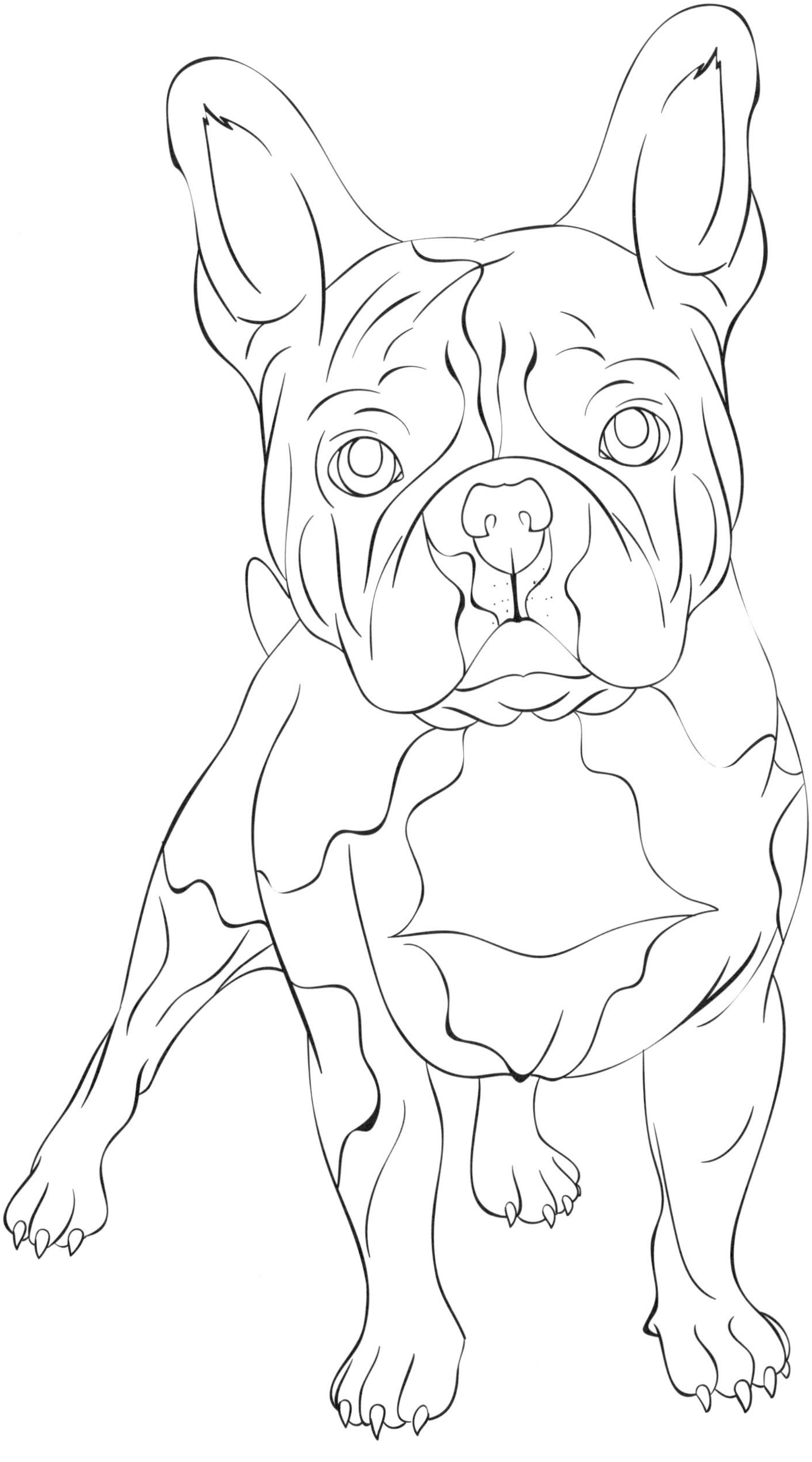

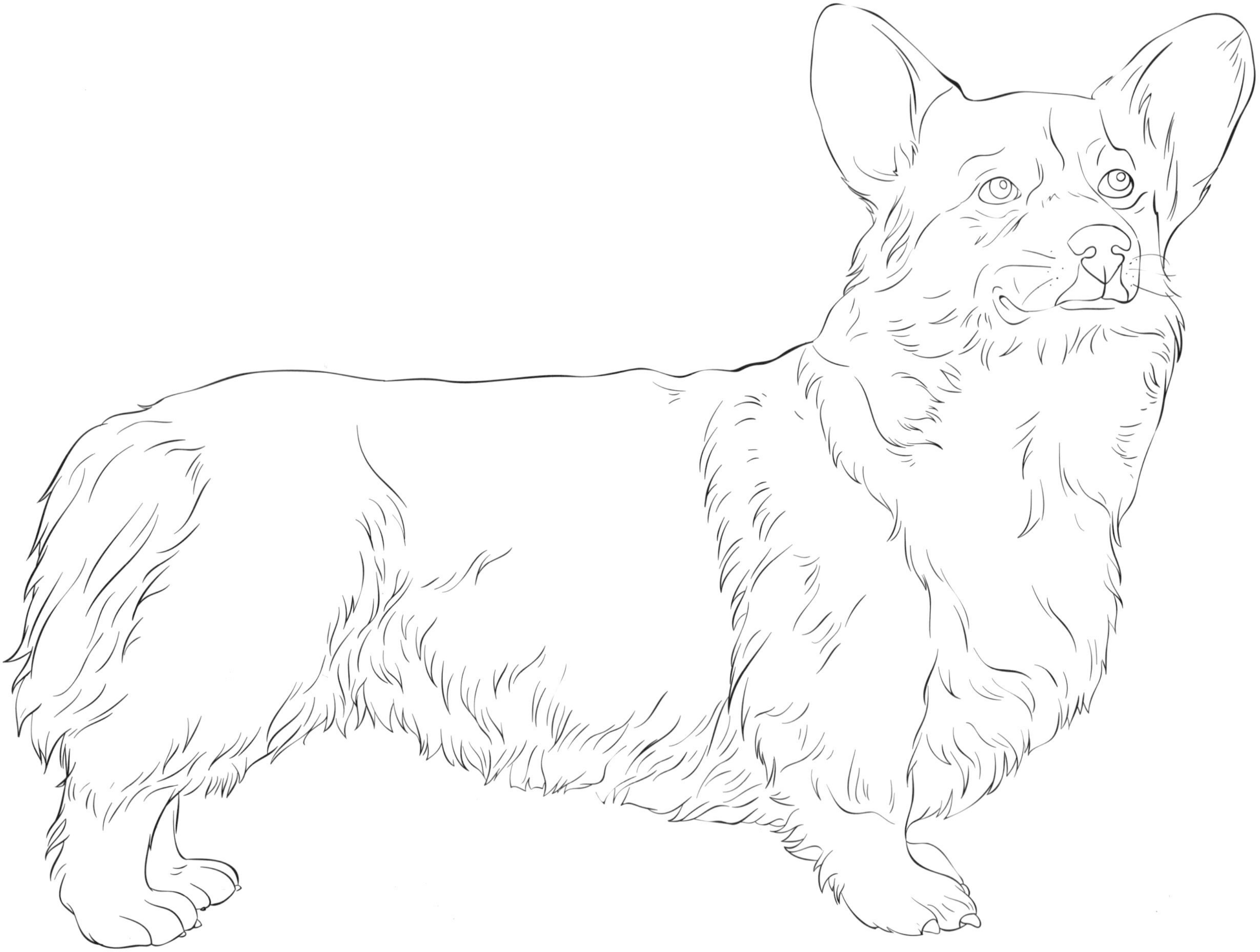

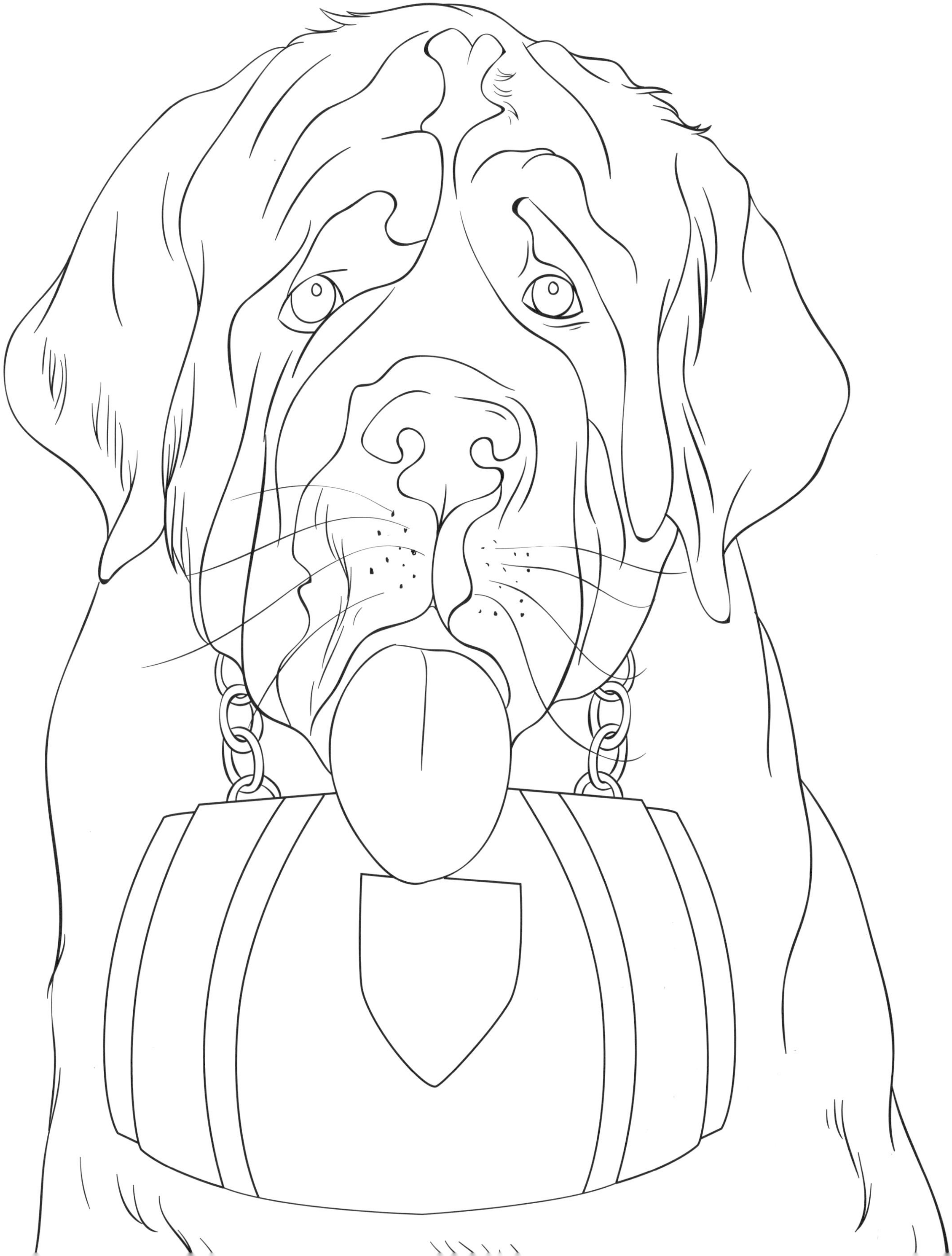

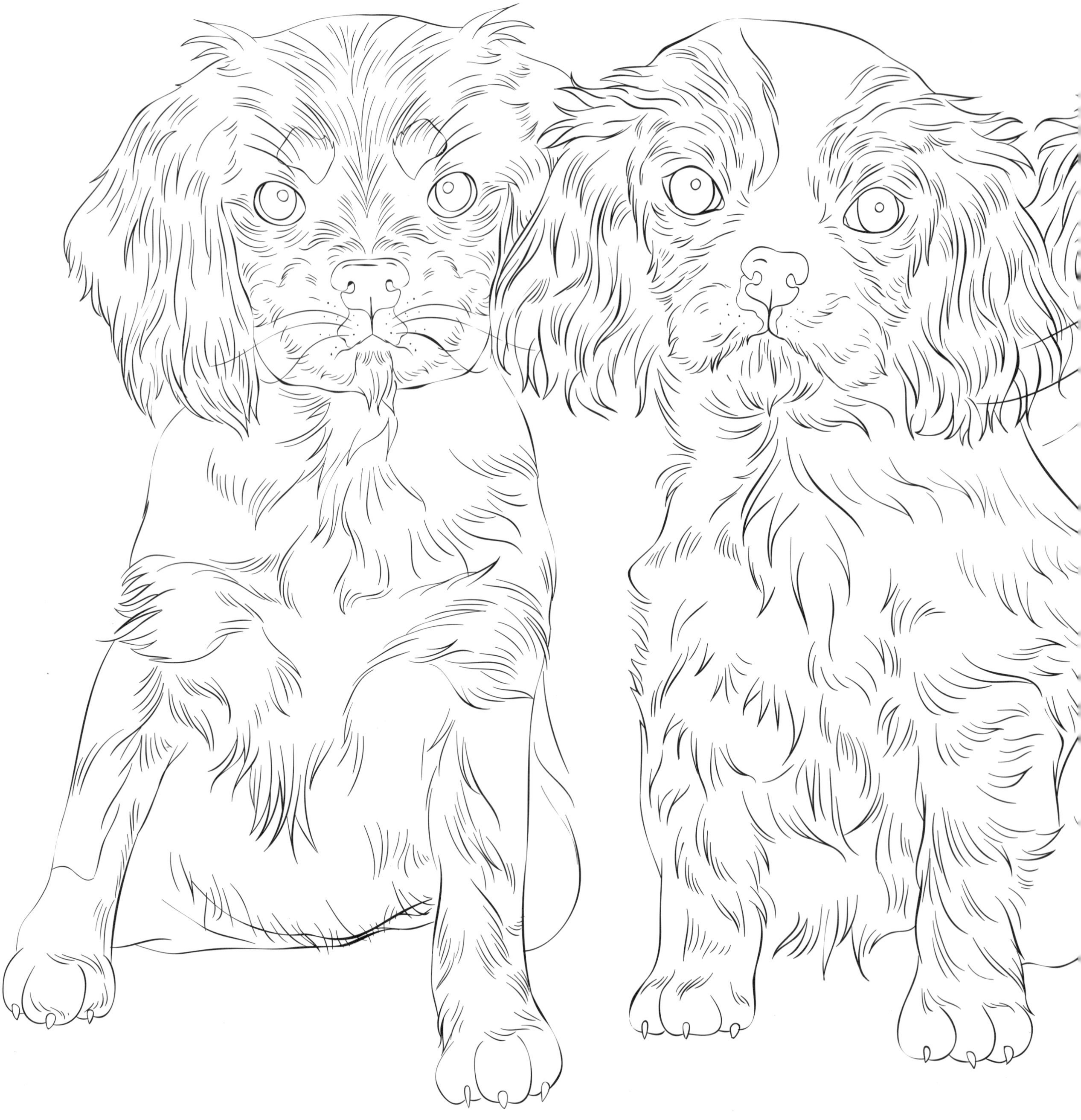

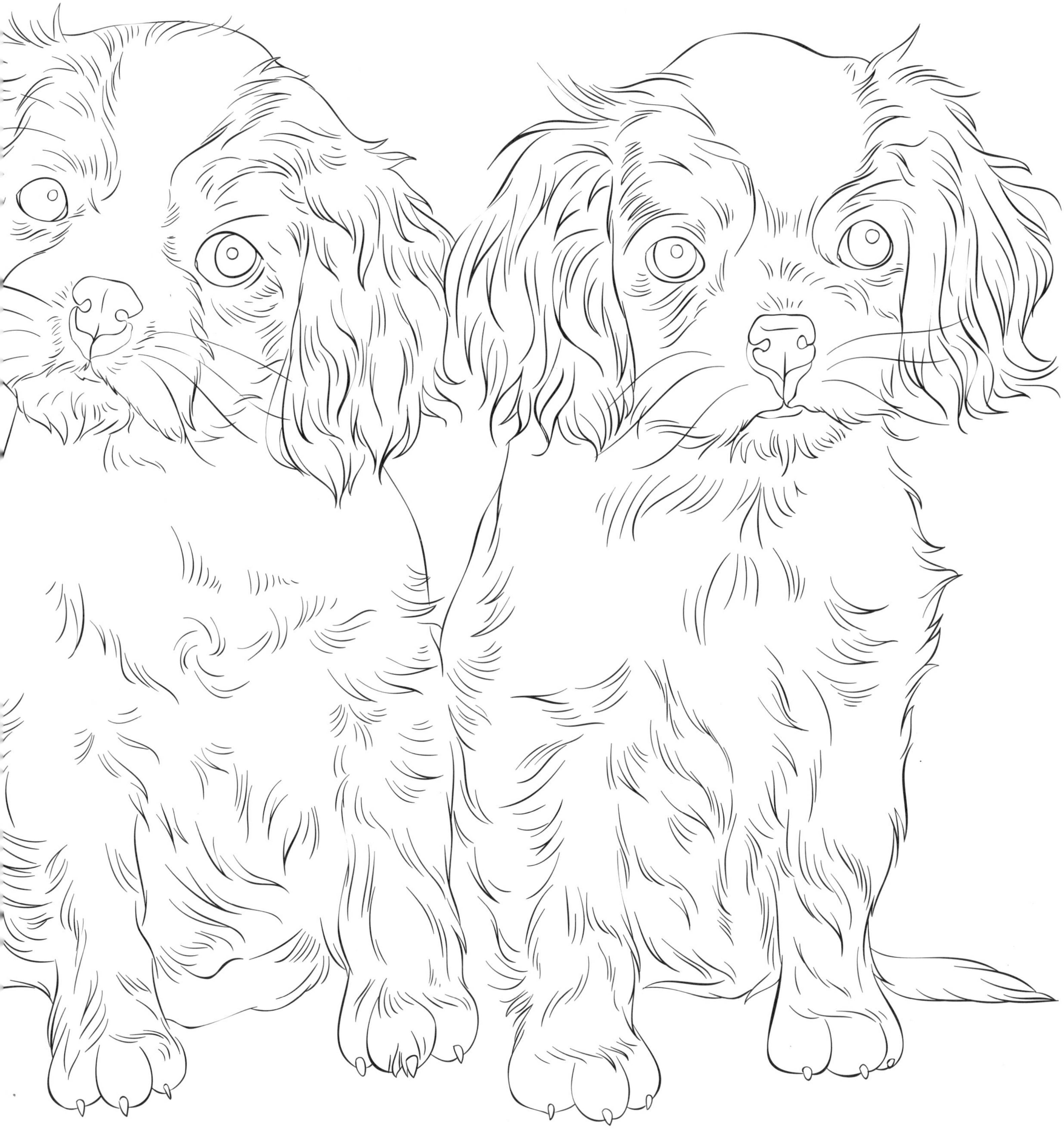

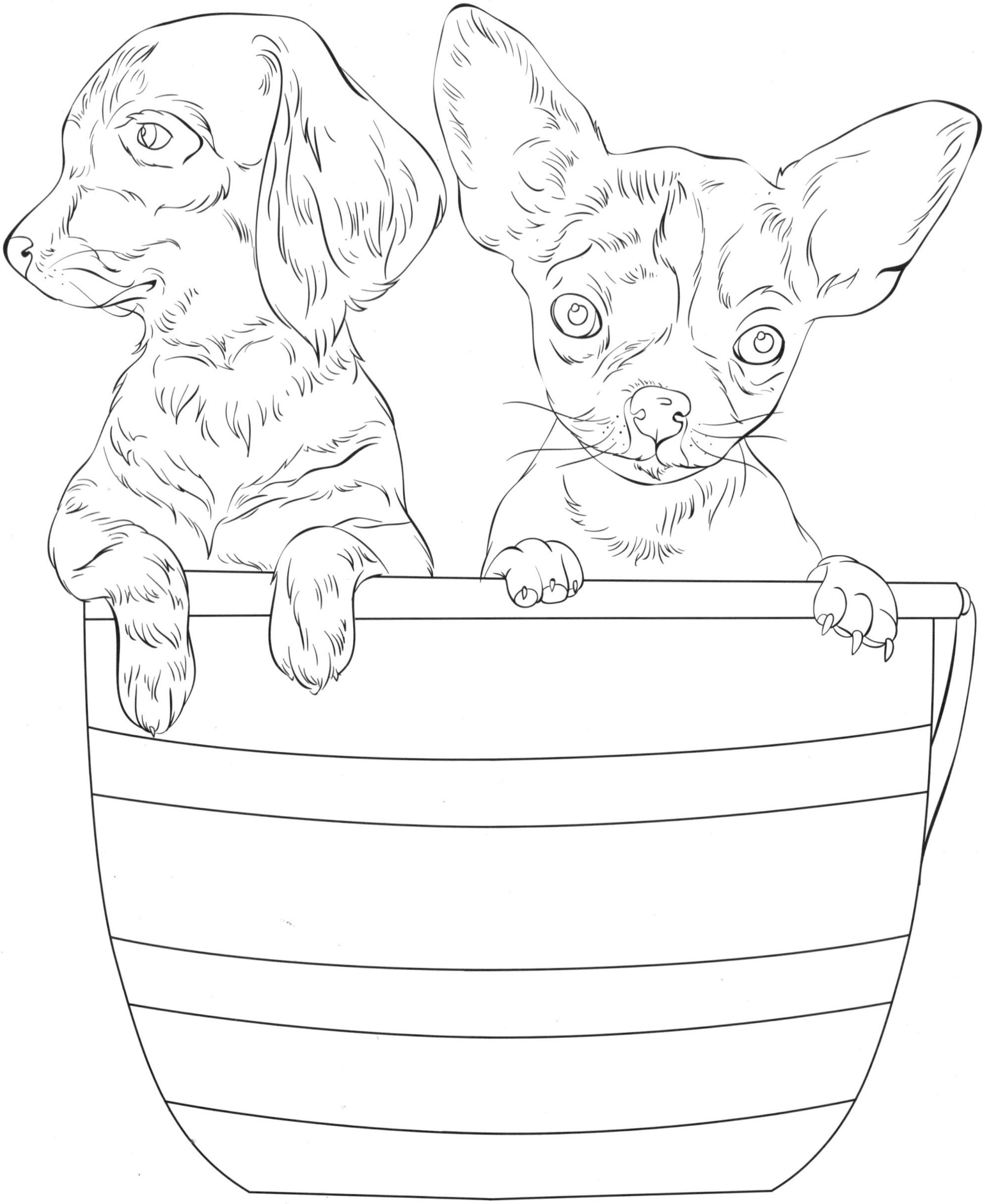